Foreign Correspondence

Foreign Correspondence

GERALDINE BROOKS

Anchor Books

DOUBLEDAY

New York   London   Toronto   Sydney   Auckland

AN ANCHOR BOOK

PUBLISHED BY DOUBLEDAY

a division of Bantam Doubleday Dell Publishing Group, Inc.
1540 Broadway, New York, New York 10036

ANCHOR BOOKS, DOUBLEDAY, and the portrayal of an
anchor are trademarks of Doubleday, a division of
Bantam Doubleday Dell Publishing Group, Inc.

Book design by Ellen Cipriano

Library of Congress Cataloging-in-Publication Data

Brooks, Geraldine.
    Foreign correspondence: a pen pal's journey from Down Under to
all over / by Geraldine Brooks. — 1st Anchor Books ed.
        p.   cm.
    1. Brooks, Geraldine. 2. Foreign correspondents—Australia—
Biography.   I. Title.
PN5516.B76A3   1998
070.4'332'092—dc21
[B]   97-15413
                                                                CIP

ISBN 0-385-48269-8

First Anchor Books Edition: January 1998

1 3 5 7 9 10 8 6 4 2

To the memory of Lawrie, and to Gloria

. . . nothing is more sweet in the end than
country and parents ever,
even when far away one lives in a fertile place . . .
—The Odyssey

CONTENTS

Part One

Part Two

ACKNOWLEDGMENTS

I would like to thank Martha Levin and Elise O'Shaughnessy for convincing me to write this book; Darleen and Michael Bungey, Miki Bratt, Sarah and David Chalfant, Charlie Conrad, Elinor Horwitz, Brian Hall, Gail Morgan and Tina Pohlman for their comments on its early drafts; Joshua Horwitz, all-purpose sage; and Sara Mauck, without whose help it wouldn't have been finished.

Above all, I would like to thank the two men in my life: Tony, who put the idea in my head and then helped to get it on the page, and Nathaniel, whose full-throated comments and occasional efforts at the keyboard made it easier to reenter the world of my own childhood.

Foreign Correspondence

⁓❧⁓

Part One

1

Post Marked

It is a hot spring day and I am in the basement of my parents' house in Sydney, sorting through tea chests. Pine floorboards creak above my head as my mother steps beside my father's bed, checking his breathing mask. The old floor is thin and while I can't make out her words I recognize the tone, its veneer of cheerfulness layered on anxiety.

From my father, propped up on pillows, I hear nothing. He barely speaks anymore. His voice—the beautiful voice that once made his living—is silenced by the simple effort of breathing. He is staring toward a picture window that frames a view of ocean through a fluttering fringe of gum leaves. But he can't see it. His eyes, almost sightless now, are the whitened blue of faded cornflowers.

When my father moved to this beach house just after his retirement, he should have had the leisure to sort his old sheet music, to work on his half-composed tunes, read his cricket books, enjoy his correspondence. Instead, he became ill that year and never found the energy even to unpack. So I have come down here to do it, because I don't think I will have the heart to face these things once he is dead.

The dirt floor of the unfinished basement is cool against my bare legs, and I take my time. Twelve years of dust has filtered through the flimsy lids. Spiders scurry away, indignant, as I disturb them.

My father squirreled away everything. There are yellowed news clippings about his career as a big-band singer in Hollywood and Hawaii in the 1930s, before he came to Australia. There are dozens of dog-eared photographs of musicians with frangipani leis lying incongruously against their tuxedos; even more of Australian army mates in slouch hats at the Pyramids, in Jerusalem's Old City, among the huge-leaved trees of New Guinea.

And there are letters, piles of them. Replies to every piece of correspondence my father ever wrote. He wrote, I realize as I unfold the brittle pages of fifty-year-old letters, to everyone. From 1931, there is a two-line note from Albert Einstein, in verse, responding to a request for permission to perform a ditty about him that my father had composed. Einstein writes: "Though somewhat silly, I don't mind—there's no objection I can find!" There is White House stationery—a 1969 reply from the chairman of the Council of Economic Advisers thanking my father for his "good letter" on interest rates. There is a 1974 response from the office of Rupert Murdoch answering my father's complaint about the creasing in his broadsheet newspapers. And a letter from an acoustical expert thanking my father for his suggestions about raising the height of a concert-hall floor to improve the way sound carries.

Each letter is a small piece of the mosaic of my father's restless mind, its strange mingling of global interests and nit-picking obsessions. Some of the replies raise questions: Why did he write to the Israeli Minister of Defense in 1976? Where is the poem he wrote about Winston Churchill that the Australian

Prime Minister thanks him for in a 1958 letter? My father is beyond answering such questions now. I have left it too late to ask.

Near the bottom of a tea chest is a thick pile of airmail letters that raises an altogether different set of questions. Held by a withered rubber band, they are addressed, in various childish handwritings, to me. As I pull them out and blow the dust off, I recognize them as letters from my pen pals—from the Middle East, Europe, the United States.

I stare at them, puzzled. It was my mother who saved our school report cards, our drawings and poems, old toys and memorabilia. While I have never doubted that my father loved my sister and me, he rarely involved himself in the day-to-day business of our lives. Yet here, among his things, is more than a decade of my correspondence, from 1966, when I discovered pen pals, to 1979, when my parents moved to this house.

When I wrote to these pen pals, in the late 1960s and 1970s, my family inhabited a very small world. We had no car, had never set foot on an airplane and, despite my father's American relatives, never thought of making an international telephone call.

In the evenings, families in our neighborhood would gather on the front verandas of their houses and wait for the "southerly buster"—the big thunderstorm that would break the heat, lay the dust and leave the air cool enough to allow sleep.

I was waiting, too. Waiting for something to happen, and wishing that I lived in a place where something did. Except for relentless coverage of the British royal family, Australian newspapers paid little attention to foreign places. The nightly TV news was more likely to lead with the coliform bacteria count at Bondi Beach than the body count in Vietnam. Yet, at school, our history books were filled with tales of elsewhere. The Great Men—and they were all men, in those days—were British,

American, German, French. I was aware from religion class that a few women had made it to greatness via sainthood, but they came from even more distant-sounding places—St. Theresa of Avila, Bernadette of Lourdes. A St. Margaret of Melbourne or a Diane of Dubbo was clearly out of the question.

My father's escape was the yellow-painted metal mailbox on a post by the privet hedge. Almost every day it contained a letter for him from somewhere else—flimsy aerograms or heavy bond paper with official-looking seals. At the age of ten I learned that it was possible for me, too, to write to strangers and have them write back to me. Suddenly, I could see a way to widen my world by writing away to all the places where I imagined history happened and culture came from. When the letters came back from Vaucluse in France or Maplewood in New Jersey, I studied the foreign images on the stamps and dreamed myself into the lives of the writers.

And now I have their letters again in my hands. I sit in the basement, reading, as the light slowly fades and the surf thuds on the nearby beach. Oldest of all, nibbled around the edges by silverfish, are the letters from my very first pen pal, a twelve-year-old girl nicknamed Nell who lived just across town, and in a different world.

Better preserved are the more recent letters from my American correspondent Joannie, to whom I wrote for more than fifteen years. She became my distant, teenage soulmate and taught me how evanescent, and how enduring, such a friendship can be. Her letters give me glimpses of my girlish self. "Do you know what the control mice died of?" she asks, reminding me of my grandiose and doomed attempt, at the age of fourteen, to alleviate world hunger by proving the edibility of garden weeds. I'd forgotten that I once knew how to write the words "Live

Long and Prosper" in the original Vulcan. And did I once call myself by the hideous nickname "Gez"?

The geography of this childhood correspondence has become the road map of the adult life I have lived. Joannie's letters became a magnet drawing me toward the United States. In 1982, I wrote to tell her I had won a graduate scholarship to the Columbia School of Journalism in New York.

The address of my pen pal in a little village in southern France is only a hundred miles from the other little French village, on the stony, sunlit hillside, where I married in 1984.

In my teens, I wrote to an Arab and a Jew in the Middle East. Twenty-five years later, I arrived in Cairo on a hot autumn night to spend six years covering the Middle East as a reporter. From foreign correspondent to Foreign Correspondent: I have become the envelope full of words flying around the world.

But I know so little about these people who shaped my vision of the world. How has the reality of their lives matched the fantasies I projected on them from the safe harbor of my Sydney girlhood? I begin to wonder if it's possible to track down forty-year-old adults using only the childish letters they wrote half a lifetime ago. Gently gathering the fragile correspondence with its faded addresses, I decide that one day soon I will try to find out.

2

Return Address

⁓෨Ⓒ๑⁓

Now, when I do not live there any more, Sydney floats in my imagination like Atlantis. The sunlit harbor is everywhere, its glittering fingers poking into clusters of coral-red roofs.

In the argot of geologists, Sydney is a drowned river valley. The ocean has poured over the ancient pathways of inland waters, flooding the bottomlands and leaving only the high ground exposed. Instead of a gentling from hill to valley to shore, earth and water collide abruptly. Sheer sandstone cliffs confront the glassy breakers of the Pacific, and high knolls plunge straight into deep inlets.

From the air, the land looks like two gnarled hands reaching for each other across a watery abyss. On one finger, the skyscrapers of the central business district rise suddenly like an ostentatious ring. That knot of glitter loosens into a mesh of tiny cottages and terrace houses, then to the sprawl of red-roofed bungalows punctuated by the aqua oblongs of backyard swimming pools. In those backyards, rainbow lorikeets dangle, bright as Christmas lights, from the branches of red gum trees. Winter wattle blooms golden against a crisp blue sky.

This primary-colored paradise is a trick of homesick memory. This Sydney exists, to be sure. But it is not the city in which I grew up. I was born on Bland Street, Ashfield, and the background color of my childhood is the ashy gray of the high, weathered fences that marked out each quarter-acre lot. Summers bleached the backyard grass colorless and dried it until it crunched underfoot. Beyond the fence, our treeless street melted in the sun, the black asphalt bubbling.

We lived in one of the lower-middle-class neighborhoods that ooze westward from the coast across a baking plain to the city's perimeter at the foot of the Blue Mountains. We were part of a sprawl that extended over six hundred uninterrupted square miles and housed a quarter of Australia's population.

From the rim of that flat plain, I had no sense of my city's dramatic topography. The harbor that now so dominates my image of the city does not figure in any of my early memories. Perhaps it is because young children are unmoved by scenery of all sorts, their focal point always on the faces of the people around them. Dimly, I knew that the harbor existed, because it was where they were building the fanciful, toylike Opera House. My mother and her friends sometimes shared a ticket in the Opera House lottery. If they won, I supposed, we would get title to the building, and all go to live under the soaring white sails. Perhaps I would be allowed to use the smooth, plunging roofs as slippery-slides.

We did not go to the city or the beach. Because we had no car, even short journeys loomed in family discussions like epic treks. Besides, my parents were too busy on weekends fixing gutters and fighting rising damp in our Victorian terrace house.

From the outside, the Bland Street terrace was a picturesque pair of houses linked by a common center wall. A cake-decoration trim of cast-iron balconies squiggled its lacy way across the facade. But the charm was all exterior. Inside, the rooms were dank in winter, stifling in summer, the few windows taking no account of the Mediterranean-style climate of the new city in which it had been set down. Its design wasn't meant for Sydney. Like a good part of the city's population of that time, the terrace style had been lifted straight from cold, crowded cities such as London or Dublin.

While my mother battled broken sash cords and crumbling plaster, my father hacked away at the tangles of morning glory in the overgrown garden or slapped sealer on the rusty iron roof. Weekends were the only times I really saw him. Weekdays, he left early for his job as a proofreader on a daily newspaper. Early in the morning while I was still drowsy, he was a fleeting scent of Californian Poppy hair oil and a sweet, sharp taste of sugary black coffee in a hurried goodbye kiss. Most nights, he was out until way past my bedtime, singing at nightclubs, in recording-studio sessions, or on the radio.

But on weekends he would be home: up the dizzying extension ladder, shirtless, tanned, glistening with sweat. His unlined face and firm torso looked like a young man's. He never walked anywhere; he bounced like a boy. He liked to sprint across busy streets, dodging cars with the graceful swoops of a matador. Yet by the time I was two, he was already fifty.

My mother, in her mid-thirties, was the adult in our lives. Weekdays, I was her shadow, roaming the rooms of the big house while my sister Darleen, an unfathomable eight years older, was away all day at school. I would climb upstairs to the iron-lace balcony, peering through its arabesques at the street below.

It was through that filigree that the outside world gradually came into focus. Every afternoon, in the garden of the monastery adjacent to the Catholic school across the road, a black-soutaned figure paced back and forth, reading his Office from a small prayer book. The sight of this slender cleric soothed me: I thought he was God. I was glad we had him so handy.

We lived on Bland Street during the bland years of Australia's history. Like the 1950s in the United States, the postwar years in Australia were a timid, conservative time. My parents' generation had been wracked by the Depression and the war. Happy to be alive and employed, most of them were too exhausted to contemplate change. The right-wing government that came to power in 1949 stayed in office for more than twenty years. Its leader was Robert Menzies, an Anglophile who felt more at home at a palace ceremony in London than he did in his own country. Returning from England in 1941, he wrote in his journal that "a sick feeling of repugnance grows in me as I near Australia."

His pro-British, pro-monarchy rhetoric infected us all with the sense that we were second-raters—inferior convict stock who should continue to look to the culture and history of our colonizer rather than try to forge an identity of our own. So, instead of admiring the spiky beauty of native grevillias and the hazy, bottlebrush-shaped blooms of callistimon, we planted our gardens with English primroses and watched them wilt in the heat. We decorated our walls with portraits of Queen Elizabeth and prints of landscapes by Constable and Turner. At Christmas, when overripe papayas fell from our backyard tree with a wet splat, we sweated our way through a dinner designed for a European winter solstice, with dried fruit on the table and pudding flamed in brandy for dessert.

We had no idea how to use our benign climate to grow a wider variety of produce than our English and Irish forebears had known. At the greengrocer, lettuce meant iceberg. A seafood dinner meant fried fish and chips—never the cheap, plentiful produce of the harbor, the calamari or delicious, nutty-fleshed crustaceans called Balmain bugs. Richer families sent their children to be educated at private institutions with names like "The King's School" and "Scotch College" where elocution teachers vainly tried to round out the flattened vowels of a Cockney and Celtic heritage. The country's premiere institution of higher learning, the University of Sydney, stated its mission of aping Oxford and Cambridge in its motto, Sedare Mens Edam Mutato (Same Place Different Skies). It didn't even have a chair of Australian literature until the 1960s. At sports events and official functions, we stood for the playing of our national anthem: "God Save the Queen."

In a city where even the governor's residence had been built facing the wrong way—its big windows orient south, waiting in vain to catch the light of a sun that in our hemisphere moves through the northern sky—it was no wonder that our Bland Street terrace house was a misplaced piece of Victorian England. For the five years after I was born, my parents worked on the house until they finally had it in shape to sell. With the profit, we moved a few miles farther west to a neighborhood named Concord, into a smaller, newer, cookie-cutter cottage designed at the time Australia's states achieved federation in 1901. A cool, tiled porch shaded the front door, which opened on a central hallway. Inside, the hall divided four rooms two by two and then emptied into a dining room and kitchen running lengthways across the back. An enclosed veranda had been added beyond.

It was another bland street of liver-brick bungalows, identically designed, marching in lockstep away from the grand homes that lined the harbor. As the neighborhoods spread west, they gradually became less affluent, ending with the newer, flimsier fibro houses going up on the distant plain. The farther west, the hotter the summers, the fewer the trees and the longer the journey back to the harbor and wide scalloped beaches.

In the fine distinctions of Sydney social geography, Concord was "inner west," denied ocean breezes or harbor views, yet not without patches of period charm. Our house was a bargain because it was "in the road"—slated for eventual destruction for a planned western expressway. But the city planners hadn't figured on my mother, a tireless lobbyist. Her decade of campaigning would eventually help to get the highway rerouted and net the windfall that would allow my parents to move to the beautiful northern beaches.

For my mother, the Concord house was a dream. Sunlit and impeccably maintained, its lack of stairs, its clean dry plaster and its pale green wall-to-wall carpet signaled the end of the endless drudgery imposed by the Bland Street terrace. The garden, too, was orderly: no rampant lantana or morning-glory vines. Just clipped privet hedges and an expanse of crew-cut buffalo grass, with severely pruned orange, mandarin and apricot trees lining the gray wood fences.

But there was more to this move than two people looking for fewer chores. I think that something in the house's tidy, foursquare proportions spoke to a wish that both my parents shared: a wish for a simpler, more stable life than either of them had known.

As a Depression child, my mother Gloria had lived through her parents' loss of their house and the necessary migrations that followed, from one temporary lodging to another. Her own glamorous, relentlessly social mother had never been at home much, wherever they were living. Throughout her childhood, Gloria's dream had been to have a mother who stayed in the same chair in a familiar room, busy with her knitting. The Concord house looked to her like a fine place to knit.

• • •

It's less easy to say how it looked to my father.

Lawrie Brooks was an Australian by accident. Born in California in 1907, he'd been twenty years old when he saw Al Jolson in the legendary first talkie, *The Jazz Singer*. Lawrie had a beautiful clear tenor voice, so while he worked in a steel mill he took singing lessons. With the help of vocal scholarships, good looks and good luck, he made his way into the white-tie world of the big bands. He sang at the grand hotels—the St. Francis, the Biltmore and the Royal Hawaiian—with the bands of Johnny Noble, Harry Owens, Hal Grayson, Jimmie Grier and Jay Whidden. In Hollywood, he appeared on the same bill as Eddie Cantor, Burns and Allen and the Downey Sisters. He sang for the Academy Awards at the Biltmore Bowl.

In 1938 he set off with the Whidden band for a season in Australia. When the band's engagements in the cities ended, my father decided to stay on with another band, to take a look at the Outback. But flash floods turned the tour into a disaster. The stress, on top of the long, hard-drinking nights on the road, put Lawrie briefly in hospital with a stomach ailment. While he was there, the band leader absconded with his pay. Lawrie was stranded, without the fare to get back to the United States.

While trying to earn his passage home, he developed a taste for Australia's strong beer, dull cricket and intense, male-bonding mateship. So firm were the friendships that when his Aussie musician mates joined up in the Australian Infantry Forces the day that France fell to the Nazis, he decided to enlist with them, rather than with the U. S. Army. They formed an entertainment unit and toured the front lines in the Middle East and the Pacific. Corporal Brooks spent his war singing in Egyptian sandstorms and slowly sinking thigh-deep into New Guinea jungle mud.

Back in Sydney in the postwar years before the arrival of

television, radio was Australia's glamor industry and Lawrie became one of its stars. He soon met Gloria Van Boss, a radio-station publicist with a deft touch for getting celebrities on the front page of the daily papers.

Lawrie Brooks proposed to Gloria Van Boss on a Sydney tram in 1946. Before she gave her answer, he insisted on telling her the story of his life. As the tram rattled along, he unfolded a tale of almost forty hard-lived years.

It was a story she kept to herself. My father's past remained a mystery to me, revealed gradually, and only in accidental fragments.

"Daddy, who's this?" It is a still, sleepy Sunday afternoon in 1962. Darleen is out; my mother is napping. Looking for some-thing to do, I have followed my father to the back veranda, where he is trying to organize a closetful of paperwork.

Most of the pictures in our family album are black and white. So the colored snapshot that slides from amid the papers on the shelf catches my eye. The woman in the photograph wears a strapless sheath of scarlet sequins. Nobody dresses like that in Concord. I turn the picture this way and that, trying to figure out what is holding the lady's dress up. I decide it must be the way the top of her body sticks out in front, perpendicular as a shelf.

As my father takes the photograph, his eyebrows rise in surprise, as if it is something he didn't expect to find. He says quietly, "That's Ruby. She's someone I knew in America." He is about to say more but thinks better of it. He places the picture in his pocket and goes on shuffling papers. Thirty years later, when I sort through the tea chests that contain his life's memorabilia, that photo is nowhere to be found.

. . .

Gloria learned all about Ruby during that tram ride in 1946, along with other names that were never discussed again. The week after she accepted his proposal, she was quietly taken aside by my father's fellow musicians, all of whom warned her that, while Lawrie was "the best mate a bloke could have," she'd be out of her mind to marry him.

But they underestimated her. Not long after their marriage, my parents began a quiet withdrawal from the turbulent show business world. By the time I was five, they had turned their backs on it with stunning thoroughness. Relics of that old life lay in my dress-up cupboard. There were my father's buttery-soft black silk shirts and stiff moiré cummerbunds; my mother's shimmery, hand-beaded evening dresses and fur-trimmed pill-box hats. But the splendid creatures who had worn these clothes existed for me only in the pages of our photo albums. The father I knew wore serviceable polyester. My mother never seemed to think about clothes at all.

The last step in their retreat from celebrity came when my father ended his thirty-year singing career. When friends asked about his decision to quit, my father laughed and said that fifty-four was old enough for a pop singer. But he still looked uncannily youthful. My mother used to joke that she needed every day of the twelve-year gap in their ages.

The friends who questioned his decision had seen the handsome tuxedoed man and heard the soaring voice. What they hadn't seen was what came before the performances, or what came after.

Perhaps nothing unnerves a child so much as perceiving fear in a parent. Before my father went off at night to singing engagements I would crawl under the dressing table to play with the box of studs and shiny cuff links he wore with his tuxedo. When I noticed his hands shake as he tied his bow tie, my own four-year-old stomach would contract with dread. Lawrie Brooks, who had sung before thousands, had stage fright. As he kissed me goodbye at the door, he would be trembling. I was asleep long before he returned. But in the middle of the night I would wake to hear him in the bathroom, retching.

After he gave up singing, Lawrie became a creature of unalterable habit, as if he needed a rock-solid routine to compensate for all the chaos that had come before. Nothing was too minute to have a set of rules. Old soap scraps had to be molded into the new bars with sculptural precision. Forks had to be washed up first. In the fruit bowl citrus had to be quarantined from other fruit lest it hasten rotting.

The quotidian round of work, pub and domesticity somehow seemed to be enough to make up for the loss of music in his life. For me, it meant that I heard his wonderful voice mostly on the old 78rpm records we kept in a cupboard. It was a tall stack—sixty recordings in all, from corny Hawaiian tunes such as "I've got a little grass skirt for my little grass shack in Hawaii," to Irish-tenor ballads and his own favorites—the jazz improvisations in which the glide of his voice eased around the notes of the clarinets and saxophones as if it were just another instrument under a musician's expert control.

Sometimes, when he came to church for someone's wedding or confirmation, he would join in singing a hymn. I loved to watch the heads turn as his rich tenor soared into the church's high dome, drowning the woolly chorus of ordinary voices.

I started school the year my father stopped singing. It was a scorching midsummer day at the end of January, and the blue cotton of the new school tunic prickled me all over. Even under the big straw brim of the school hat, the sun's dazzle hurt my eyes. The empty brown school case felt heavy as it banged against my aching knees.

I was in the playground at morning recess when my mother and father arrived to take me home. The doctor had called them with the results of a test that showed I had serious blood anomalies. The illness had no precise diagnosis, but the doctor suspected rheumatic fever. To reduce strain on my heart, he said, I wasn't to be allowed to walk at all. So my father carried me the seven blocks home. My mother called in the country's preeminent pediatrician, Sir Lorimer Dods. This tall, silver-haired gentleman was as baffled as the local doctor. He ordered me to stay in bed and lie as still as I could. For more than a month I wasn't allowed to get up even to go to the toilet.

The next three years passed in a blur of recurring fevers, where familiar voices echoed unrecognizably and synesthesia made my father's jazz records pour over me in bands of bright chrome yellow. Since then, my father's beloved jazz has been the only kind of music I can't bear, and certain tones of yellow make me feel as if I'm running a temperature of 103.

When I knew I was becoming ill again, I dreaded breaking the news to my mother. Trying to warn her gently, I'd scan my vocabulary for the least alarming words I knew. "Mummy, I think I've got just an eentsy-weensy, tiny little bit of a sore throat," I'd say, and she would turn to me, her face changing in an instant like a theatrical mask falling from comic grin to tragic grimace. She would reach for my forehead to feel for fever and her palm would land on my already hot skin like a block of ice. And then I would be back in bed, on the edge of delirium, my body feeling like an aching bruise.

The bursts of illness always ended the same way: I would wake from a deep afternoon sleep in my parents' bed to find the fever broken, able to feel the delicious cool breeze blowing through the front window. As it lifted the filmy white curtain, I would stretch my no longer aching limbs and luxuriate in the simple pleasure of wellness. Out the window, the red Christmas bush vibrated against the clear blue sky, and I could notice again how beautiful it was.

The days of recuperation that followed were magical times when I basked in my mother's undivided attention. Together, we explored a tiny world—the garden, the neighborhood—that her imagination made vast.

My mother had been raised at a time when most Australian girls left school at fourteen. And even those few years of schooling had been disrupted by the Depression and a stepfather with no head for business who dragged her from rural town to rural town, as he tried to sell shares in failing companies to people with no spare cash for the weekly rent.

She missed huge slabs of formal education, but compensated by joining the library of every country town in which they paused. She devoured books by the armload. Her stepfather, a dreamy Dutch immigrant, had arrived in Australia as a nineteen-year-old without a word of English. He had taught himself the language while working as an itinerant fruit picker, and by the time he met my grandmother was able to woo her with his own florid sonnets. My grandmother had grown up amid a blarney-filled family of Irish immigrants who loved to spin stories.

With place and possessions uncertain, my mother put her faith in words. She knew that a poem, once memorized, could never be taken from her. One of her set pieces was a long, funny and exhausting verse called "Packing." This proved such a big hit with the convent-school teachers that they'd ask her to recite it when the regional school inspector visited. At one point, my mother was changing schools so frequently that the same inspector had to sit through two renditions of "Packing." During the first performance, he laughed heartily. During the second, he smiled politely. But when he saw my mother's bright, eager face about to launch into an encore at yet a third school, he turned pale, made some excuse to the teacher and backed out of the classroom.

The nuns despaired of my mother. "Gloria," chided one, "all you can do is talk, and nobody is ever going to pay you to do that." The nun was wrong. Gloria Van Boss was still in her teens when she became a radio announcer.

If my father's past was a mysterious blur, my mother's memories were often more vivid to me than my own. When she talked of an Outback town named Boorowa, my eyes narrowed against the dry dust of its orange dirt roads. I could taste the flesh of the sun-warmed apricots as she pulled them from the tree. I imagined my own tender, well-shod feet as brown and splayed as hers after a barefoot summer running wild in the paddocks and dried-up river beds.

Boorowa was the refuge of my mother's Depression childhood. When her stepfather's tenuous work dried up or the food bills got too high, she would be bundled off on a train to her grandmother Bridget O'Brien and the half dozen aunts who still lived on the baking plains of western New South Wales. There was no money out there, but there was always a freshly butchered sheep or enough eggs from the henhouse to feed another child. One of the aunts would find a space for her somewhere, tucked into a bed with two or three cousins.

The Boorowa stories were the Icelandic sagas of my childhood sickbed. I lived among the characters of this ongoing narrative until they became more real to me than the neighbors on our suburban street. There were few children in our neighborhood, and none my age. Rarely well enough to go to school for more than three or four days at a time, I made no close friends among my classmates. My older sister Darleen was a glamorous but elusive figure who inhabited a realm I entered only when, in a burst of noblesse oblige, she permitted me to hover at the edges of her teenage doings. So my best friend was the other lonely, watchful outsider: the child my mother had been all those years ago in Boorowa.

The O'Briens came to Australia from the misty green country around Limerick. If they felt despair in 1844 when they first set eyes on the hard, bleached land around Boorowa, there is no record of it. None of them could write.

Bridget O'Brien, my great-grandmother, was a formidable Irish Catholic bigot who raised her six daughters to wait hand and foot on their three spoiled brothers. Less than five feet tall and full of energy, delivering babies with no training and no medical backup, she brought most of Boorowa into the world and never lost a mother or an infant. Yet she told her daughters so little of the facts of life that my pregnant grandmother expected her first baby to pop out of her navel.

Early in the mornings, when the manic chorus of Outback birds woke Gloria at dawn, she would come upon Grandma O'Brien in the kitchen, cradling a newborn. "I found her in the parsley patch," Grandma O'Brien would say. My mother, avid to find an infant of her own, would force herself awake even earlier the next day, scouring the parsley patch until her nightgown was soaked with dew. But even when she rose before dawn, Grandma O'Brien had always just beaten her to the new baby.

In the late afternoons, after the local grazier's sheep had been dipped or his fences mended, Grandfather O'Brien would return home dog-tired and settle into his favorite chair on the big white veranda. He had never been to school, so my mother would read him the newspaper. Mostly, he liked to hear the form guide for the next day's races. As she read the names of the horses and the details of their last starts, he would hone his pocket knife until it was sharp enough to glide through paper, then use it to peel thin slivers of pipe tobacco from a plug black and dense as licorice.

Because she was a girl, Gloria got scant attention from Grandma O'Brien. But unnoticed herself, she noticed everything. She eavesdropped on the farmhands bringing their wives for lying in. "Sure and you can come back tomorrow around lunchtime and the baby'll be about arriving then," Grandma O'Brien would say. "Oh no, Grandma O'Brien," the youth would reply. "The baby can't come at lunchtime. I was never home at lunchtime."

Gloria hid under tables to eavesdrop on her uncles and aunts. When drunken Uncle Oscar sang a Latin requiem over the corpses of his empty gin bottles, she could barely stifle her giggles. She noted the breathtakingly risky behavior of the unmarried aunts, planning illicit romances. One of them, caught in a compromising situation with a strange man, uttered a sentence that amused her as a little girl, even though it was years before she knew why. "It's quite all right, sister, he's a traveling salesman" became a code phrase in our household any time someone gave an unconvincing excuse for questionable behavior.

My grandmother, Bridget's fifth daughter, was the most beautiful of the O'Brien girls. Towering over her tiny, wizened mother, her looks were more Spanish than Irish. Tall, with high cheekbones, lustrous hair and flashing eyes, she learned early that her allure was a ticket out of that dusty town. In her haste to get away, she chose poorly. Her first husband walked out on her at the beginning of the Depression, leaving her with two babies.

By the time I knew my grandmother, she was an entirely urban person. Her talonlike red-lacquered fingernails looked as if they'd never touched soil. Her luxurious hair, silvered with age, was coifed beyond the reach of a tousling breeze. A single fly would drive her to distraction. The entire household had to mobilize until its slaughter was effected.

In every urban family's history, there is a generation that loses its contact with the land. In our family, that generation was mine. Grandpa and Grandma O'Brien died years before I was born. Like my grandmother, the other aunts and uncles gradually drifted to the city. Strangers moved into the big house with the white verandas, and my mother's visits to Boorowa ended.

Occasionally a character from my mother's sagas would turn up in Concord, transported there as if by some kind of magical time machine. They had wonderful names: Auntie Pansy, Auntie Maisey, Uncle Curl. One day, to my delight, we returned from a shopping trip to find legendary Uncle Oscar passed out on the front veranda, dead drunk and short of a place to sleep it off.

But the huge spaces, the deep silences, the vast paddocks free of road rules and stranger danger could never be transported to the black-bitumen blocks of suburban Concord. That great dark mass of movement from country to city is made up of little specks like me: children who don't have any land left to visit, except in their parents' memories.

My mother's imagination expanded my small world far beyond the quarter acre contained by our gray fences. "Let's tour our estate," she would say, and we would, lingering to learn the stories that each plant or rock had to tell. We studied the spent shells of cicadas, the nests of bulbuls and the neatly woven, dew-jeweled spiderwebs.

She showed me how a daisy seemed to have a face, and an upended azalea bloom looked like a flouncy evening gown. You could "dress" the daisy in the azalea and send her to an imaginary ball. Our garden became my parallel universe. I divided the yard into countries and then plotted elaborate fates for their inhabitants. England was the narrow, damp side passage that the sun never quite reached. The potholed driveway on the other side of the house could be converted, with the help of the garden hose, into a riverine state that I somehow decided was Romania. The shadeless, empty expanse of buffalo grass from the kitchen door to the back fence was, of course, Australia. But the front yard—my mother's busy, colorful, formal flower garden—was France.

France had the fanciest fashions. Its daisy-faced women wore flamboyant hibiscus and petunia gowns. France's inhabitants also got the game's best plots, since the east-facing front garden was the most pleasant place to play. There were court intrigues, complicated romances, diplomatic wrangling, wars with England or Romania. In the backyard, Australia slumbered on, baking in the westerly afternoon heat, good for an occasional saga of ill-fated exploration in which the sun-ruddied geranium-people usually died of exposure, their petals wrinkled pathetically.

Despite her own interrupted education, my mother was a natural teacher. One morning, as I was trying to argue my way out of putting on the extra layers of underwear she thought essential armor against fevers, she laughed that my talent for debate would make me a fine lawyer. "You want to hear a great woman lawyer argue?" she asked, and opened *The Merchant of Venice* to Portia's mercy speech. It became a game to see how quickly I could learn it.

Instead of dreading the monthly blood tests that monitored my illness, my mother conspired to have me look forward to them. She befriended the pathologist, who praised my bravery and told me funny stories of grown men fainting. That, of course, made me braver.

Soon I had my own set of test tubes and slides. We cleared a space for my "lab" on the back veranda, between the ironing board, the dog's basket and my father's clutter of tools and paint cans. For my birthday and the following Christmas, I got a chemistry set and a microscope. There were rock collections painstakingly labeled and summer nights on the warm tin roof, lying on my back counting meteors. If the puddle water I was examining spilled on the clean laundry or bits of copper sulfate crystal got tracked into the carpet, my mother shrugged it off.

We would watch midday movies together and critique the plot, my mother falling like a hawk on inconsistent details. When neighbors dropped by for cups of tea, I would listen unobtrusively and then, when they left, we would deconstruct the conversation, she pointing out to me the subtexts of adult motivation, duplicity and self-deception that I had missed.

She taught me to recognize cant, to appreciate satire. To cheer me up on the days I went reluctantly to school, she'd plant little notes in my lunch box parodying the overwrought style of my religion textbooks: "Precious daughter—Whilst out there in the large world today, battling against forces almost beyond your control—remember, if you will, the hope of our hearts. Keep the lamp of the future trimmed and shining with a clear white light. Your mother—who loves you. (P.S. The doctors say it's not hereditary—you'll be O.K.)"

By lunchtime, I usually needed cheering up. When my temperature was normal and my strength had returned, my mother would pack me a lamb sandwich and a snack of carrot sticks, and the two of us would set out on the short walk to the school. More mornings than not, halfway up the hill a wave of dread and nausea would overpower me, and I'd wind up by the gutter, vomiting.

On the surface, St. Mary's Infants was a pleasant little Catholic parochial school with old peppercorn trees in the playground and big-windowed classrooms. The pupils were as homogeneous a group of children as it's possible to assemble—a roll call of Anglo-Saxon and Irish names such as Butcher and Brown, Sullivan and Hamilton, Cullen and Cahill. It should have been a playful, harmonious place. But the infants' school was staffed at that time by undertrained nuns in their late teens and early twenties. Grappling with who-knows-what doubts and strains in the claustrophobic confines of the convent, these tightly wound young women were too edgy and irascible to be trusted with the care of five-, six- and seven-year-olds.

In retrospect, it's clear that the nuns thought I was spoiled. They dealt with my tears and nausea by cuts of the cane, or tried to toughen me up by seating me with the roughest group of punching, hair-pulling boys in the class.

It wasn't until I reached third grade that I had any hope at all of shedding my school phobia. Miss Callaghan, the third-grade teacher, was an experienced, grandmotherly woman with the crinkly face of an apple-head doll. As I arrived weeping at the beginning of the school year, she simply held out her arms and hugged me.

And so I passed my childhood in the vast middle ground of Australian life, in a place that had neither the postcard beauty of the dramatic coast nor the lonely drama of the Outback.

All through the long, hot days of summer, Concord snoozed in a kind of stupor. Of a weekday afternoon, with the men at work and the women in their kitchens, a stillness settled over the empty streets. Only certain sounds marked the wearing away of the hours: the tic-tic-tic of a neighbor's lawn sprinkler, the gargling call of a magpie or the thump of the dog's hind leg, scratching for fleas.

On Saturday morning, the street erupted. Lawnmowers growled up and down, gnawing their way over dozens of identical oblongs of buffalo grass. The noise passed from yard to yard as one mower shuddered to a stop and another sputtered to life, like singers picking up their parts in a round. Next door, the neighbor's boy spent the day under the hood of his car, endlessly revving its sickly engine.

Saturdays were noisy inside our house, too. All afternoon,

the flat voice of a race caller muttered from the radio, a rapid burble of horse names as incomprehensible as a Latin litany. From the television came endless sports broadcasts—the loud, coarse-voiced football announcers; the slightly hushed, more genteel cricket commentators. My father set his day to this relentless tattoo, curlicues of blue smoke from his cigarette holder marking his trail from the dining-room table where he studied the race form to his easy chair in front of the television.

All day long, I'd weave through the house to the sound-tracks of my father's passions:

". . . and at tea, Australia is one for fifty-six, with Harris caught for a duck at silly mid-on . . ."

". . . andthey'recominguupontheoutside. It'sElPresidenteby anosetoHulaLadyandhalfalengthonit'sGhostlyGrey . . ."

"YOOOOU LIT-TLE BEOOOUUDY! IT'S A GOOD ONE! RIGHT BETWEEN THE POSTS!"

When my head rang from the voices, I'd retreat to the highest branches of the backyard willow tree, the only growing thing in the garden that escaped my father's ruthless pruning. Hidden in its green tresses, I would read books published in Britain and wonder what "frost" looked like, or why writers used expressions like "cold as the grave" when our relatives were buried in cemeteries where the hard red earth was hot as a kiln.

I was ten when the yellow mailbox became my way to find out.

3

Little Nell

My first pen pal came to me by way of the Sunday paper.

On Sundays, our neighborhood quieted as if someone had thrown a blanket over it. It was a stillness different in kind from the weekday lull of the lonely afternoons. This was a peopled silence, like the self-conscious hush of a crowd in a library.

Sunday's sounds were the sputtering fat of the lamb leg roasting in the oven, the thud of my mother's knife on the chopping board as she prepared a mountain of vegetables, and the rustle of the thick Sunday papers as my father turned the pages. In the street outside, the neighbors passed by on their way to Mass, their Sunday high heels clip-clipping on the concrete footpath.

In our street, only the women went to Mass; the men stayed in bed with the newspapers or sat by the fridge with a beer. Outwardly, my family fitted the mold of the local Catholic community. I went to Mass with my mother and sister while my father stayed at home. But despite the family's apparent conformity, I knew that there was something wrong with this picture.

My father didn't go to Mass with us because he wasn't a Catholic, and that set him perilously apart from the other fathers who didn't go because they couldn't be bothered. Those fathers could be forgiven at confession, or at a last-ditch, deathbed repentance. According to the nuns, non-Catholics like my father were heading to hell. At best, they were doomed to languish in limbo, which sounded a lot like spending eternity in a pediatrician's waiting room, keeping company with all the little babies who died before they could be baptized.

Every night I finished my bedtime prayers with an ardent plea for my father's imminent conversion. Bargaining a bit, I'd add that if it couldn't be imminent "could it please be before he dies and You have to burn him in eternal fire?" My father didn't seem perturbed about his long-term prospects. In fact, he looked extremely content, propped up in bed, as the three of us dressed up to go to church. He was a serene island amid the grumpy bustle as we searched for the shoe polish and fought for a turn at the iron, our moods set on edge by the pre-Communion fast that deprived us of any sustenance. My mother, who fared poorly without her morning cup of tea, was always particularly harassed, struggling to get the lunch in the oven before we set out for the church.

At the age of ten, I decked my room with the gory paraphernalia of Catholicism. An anatomically correct crucified Christ writhed over the dresser, a Sacred Heart dripped blood by the door. My brain itched with the abstract thought required by the Sacred Mysteries. Three persons one God. And the Word was made flesh. I loved the potent metaphor of the litany of Mary: Lily of the Valley, Mystic Rose, Star of the Sea. I studied the ecstatic face in her portrait and longed to be transported by divine grace.

But grace was elusive in Concord. The big church was too hot in summer, its crowd of tight-pressed bodies giving off a must of sweat and cheap perfume. The raw wooden kneelers cut into young knees, leaving angry red indentations on the unprotected flesh of bare legs.

St. Mary's Church was a huge faux-baroque folly: elements of Bernini's St. Peter's basilica scaled down and reinterpreted by a designer of suburban shopping malls. There was a gaudy lushness to it: tons of pink marble, acres of stained glass, pounds of gilt and enough graven images to trigger a new Reformation.

But within this idolaters' extravaganza the service itself had become as banal as the bingo games held in the adjacent church hall. I could just remember the Latin Mass of my early childhood; the murmured words, the priest with his back turned, doing his sacred work at the altar, the bells, the incense, the atmosphere of a divine mystery from which ordinary people were excluded.

Words like *mea culpa* and *agnus dei* and *spiritus sanctus* had sounded like a magician's chant; hocus-pocus, abracadabra. There was no such magic in the lawyerly English liturgy, muttered with the sigh of weary housewives and restless children longing to be outdoors.

> The Lord be with you.
> AND ALSO WITH YOU.
> Let us give thanks to the Lord our God.
> IT IS RIGHT AND FITTING TO DO SO.

Concord was a large parish and its priests were on the fast track to becoming bishops if they ran things right. Consequently, the men assigned there tended to be a worldly, striving lot, tough men in whom Aussie bluntness had replaced the Irish blarney. They were unabashedly political: conservative anti-Communists, disdainful of women, even though it was women's devotion that propped up the parish. Rather than offering spiritual uplift, they used their weekly sermons either to harangue us on the importance of wearing hats to Mass and obeying husbands at home, or to complain about the state of the building fund and the size of the haul from the "plate."

Each week, I waited for the priest to intone the words, "Go in peace, the Mass is ended." To which I made my only heartfelt response of the morning: "THANKS BE TO GOD."

The routine of Sunday Mass followed by Sunday roast was so firmly fixed in our family that I thought an enormous baked dinner was a religious obligation of Catholicism. Its ritual feel was heightened because it was the only meal we ate all together around the dining-room table. We sat down to succulent lamb fragrant with vinegary mint sauce, mounds of roasted onions, potatoes and pumpkin slices glistening with fat, big bowls of buttery green beans, peas and grated cabbage.

I watched, fascinated, as my father forked his already grease-drenched potatoes into a soft concave mush and anointed it with lashings of butter that would melt in the depression and form a little yellow lake. Then he piled a Matterhorn of salt at the edge of his plate and dipped each mouthful into it.

Like most families in meat-rich Australia, we enjoyed a household diet that would give a cardiologist a heart attack: lamb chops and fried eggs for breakfast; cold cuts in the lunchbox; for dinner, fat-rimmed rump steaks, thick sausages or "lamb's fry"—liver with bacon and gravy. Fridays, religion ordered us to give the meat a rest, but our fish was deep-fried in crunchy batter. Between meals, there were yummy snacks: bread and "dripping"—lamb fat spooned out of the enamel bowl that caught the drainings from the Sunday roasting pan; or, for a sweet tooth, toffee bubbling like lava until it reached stick-jaw consistency; ice-cold butter balls rolled in a crust of sugar. Now, living in the world of watery tofu and austere dribbles of cold-pressed, extra-virgin olive oil, I miss the heedless lusciousness of that food.

By the time we returned from Mass, my father would have read both newspapers cover to cover. At the table, he would share the highlights with us. He particularly admired the writing of Ross Campbell, a columnist who never split an infinitive or dangled a participle. Campbell was unusual in those days because his voice was authentically Australian at a time when most newspapers relied on syndicated columns from the British press to fill their space. Most Sundays, something Campbell wrote resonated with our own lives. It was my first childish inkling of the way writing can reveal us to ourselves. It was also my introduction to the notion that Australians had lives that were worth writing about.

He called his house Oxalis Cottage after the rampant clover-like weed that infested every Sydney suburban garden. He wrote about the vicissitudes of the "mad hour" between breakfast and school departure; the embarrassment of having inferior junk to put out on the curb on Clean-Up days.

He spoke for us in a way no one else did. When a visiting Noel Coward remarked, "I like Australia and I love those wonderful oysters," Campbell took him to task. "Though he meant it kindly," Campbell wrote, "Mr. Coward lined himself up with many other visitors who have bestowed praise on the animals here rather than the people. . . . No people have played second fiddle to their own fauna so much as Australians." It was bad enough, wrote Campbell, to be upstaged by koalas and kangaroos, but by *oysters*! "After all, when we go to other countries we take an interest in the people. We don't say: 'I liked Scotland. It has such wonderful cows.'"

For me, the most interesting of Campbell's four children was Little Nell, the daughter not much older than I was.

"Listen to this," said my father. "Sound like someone we know?" He read from the column, as Campbell described trying to tutor Little Nell in math:

" 'Three nines?'

" 'Wait a minute—it's nearly on my tongue. Twenty-eight?'

" 'No. Three nines are twenty-seven.'

" 'I was only one off.'

" 'They don't let you be one off. Three tens?'

" 'Thirty,' she said quickly. 'I'm good at tens.' "

I identified with Little Nell, because arithmetic was the only subject that didn't come easily to me. I also shared Little Nell's place in the family as younger sister to a dazzling older sibling. Nell's sister Theodora was a teenager at a time when teen culture was starting to matter. Like my sister, she was au courant with the latest music and fashions, old enough to scream at the Beatles and to hang out at the city's new folk clubs. Campbell poked gentle fun at all this. But to me, and I was sure also to my alter ego Little Nell, it was a world of unimaginable, enviable glamor.

One of his columns, called "The Follower," describing Little Nell's futile pursuit of Theodora and a visiting friend, could have been written about me and Darleen:

" 'They're mean!' she said. 'They've locked me out of their room because they're trying on their bras.' "

Like Little Nell, I seemed to spend half my life trying to get a toe into the glamorous wake of my eighteen-year-old sister. Darleen conjured style out of the unpromising air of Concord like a magician producing a bunch of flowers from a sleeve. She seemed to have been born elegant, emerging from the womb with a porcelain complexion and silky hair, while I came out with a head pushed into the shape of a tomahawk and bits of discolored skin hanging off my face. She had actually prayed for my arrival, heading to the church for nine weeks to say a novena to Our Lady to send her a baby sister. I suspect the hapless blob that arrived wasn't what she'd had in mind. For the first ten years of my life, her attitude to me was one of benign neglect.

Our worlds were separated by so much time that we had very little to do with each other.

In the oldest of our family photo albums, there is a rare childhood picture of the two of us together, taken at my sister's sixth-grade Christmas concert. It is a black and white photograph, but when I look at it I can remember exactly the fairy-floss pink of our matching party dresses. Each of us has a satin bow in her hair—my sister's pulling back a cascade of long, perfect ringlets. Mine sits askew on a basin-cut bob with a rat-gnawed asymmetry. My eyes, in the photograph, are round and luminous with excitement but my hands—twisting a knot in the skirt of my dress—betray nervousness edging on nausea.

The photographer, of course, isn't in the picture, but I can still see him as he loomed in front of us, a young man in a dark suit, flash gun in hand. "Point your toe," he said. I didn't have the faintest idea what he meant. Darleen did. The camera captures her, in all of her twelve-year-old composure, toe turned out like a prima ballerina. And there I am, my foot flopping spastically, frozen in time as a gawky four-year-old.

The camera loved Darleen. By the time this sixth-grade portrait was taken, she'd already had several years' experience as a child model. I grew up thinking it was normal to open a newspaper and find a picture of my big sister posed with a phony mother in an ad for children's wear or cake mix.

We have grown older together, trapped in the aspic of our age gap. No matter what difficult things I may master in my separate life, in my sibling life I remain the klutz who can be counted upon to spill the claret on my sister's cream silk upholstery or to be so assiduous in turning off appliances before I leave her house that I unplug everything, including the freezer. When Darleen is eighty and I'm seventy-two, the four-year-old will still be there somewhere, forever failing to point her toe.

But while it was hard to be kid sister to Darleen's dazzling presence, the eight-year gap in our ages cost her far more than it cost me. It meant that she came of age in an Australia still stifled by conservatism and misogyny. Women were invisible in Australian politics, rarely running for so much as a local council seat. No woman dared to enter that sanctum sanctorum of Aussie male social life, the public bar of the corner pub. At parties, the sexes divided almost as thoroughly as in Saudi Arabia, with no self-respecting Aussie male prepared to concede that a woman might have something to say that would interest him.

In retaliation, women concocted "bloke jokes": What's an Aussie bloke's idea of foreplay? Answer: "You awake, luv?" Why do Aussie blokes come so quickly? Because they can't wait to get down to the pub and tell their mates about it. The very existence of these jokes signaled the stirrings of women who knew that something was wrong. But it would be several more years before Germaine Greer came home to Sydney from Cambridge University, wielding words like an avenging sword and arguing almost everyone in my generation into embracing feminism.

Meanwhile, in neighborhoods like ours, girls didn't go to university. Only a rare, derided "bluestocking" aspired to anything but a makework job to fill up the interregnum between school and marriage. A 1960 study showed that less than one percent of the daughters of our social class went on to university. Instead, the girls in our circle became nuns, nurses or teachers. If none of those careers appealed, they became secretaries. Darleen had a gift with words, but she was bored stiff by our school's limited, conventional curriculum. In art, her innate talent was obvious but, to the nuns, art remained a Jane Austen-esque "accomplishment"—not a viable career option. When they gave Darleen a B for work that clearly merited a higher grade, my mother demanded to know why. "Mrs. Brooks," exclaimed the art teacher, "you know what bad types she'd meet in the art world! Surely you don't expect me to give her an A and encourage her?"

As soon as Darleen left school, her creativity expressed itself in dazzling clothes she designed herself. In the mornings, as I shrugged on the blue shift, scratchy navy sweater, felt blazer, gloves and hat of St. Mary's British-style school uniform, Darleen dressed in hot pink mini-skirts or narrow-jacketed suits and matching caps that sat fetchingly on her splendid hair.

Everyone seemed to have a crush on her, including the baker. He delivered our bread every morning, running from door to door in high-cut shorts that showed off his tanned, muscular thighs. He sped up and down the street as if trying to make a pressing deadline, but if Darleen came to the door, he lingered, rummaging among the loaves in his deep wicker basket to find the perfect one to present to her. One morning, as she paid him, one of her just-glued false eyelashes fell off and drifted gently into his basket, lost among the whole wheats and the crusty whites. The two of them knelt there in the doorway and riffled through the neighborhood's bread supply until they found it, at rest on a raisin bun.

I bathed in Darleen's reflected glitter when I could, stewed in childish envy when I couldn't. Then, gradually, she began to take an interest in me, perceiving needs that our parents missed. She made sure I got a bra before it became a schoolyard issue. She took me shopping for my first non-little-girl outfit: navy culottes with a ribbed sweater. And then, in January 1966, she brought me my first pen pal.

Darleen came home one night from her job in the *Telegraph* newspaper's circulation department with the news that her co-worker was Theodora—the columnist Ross Campbell's eldest daughter, whose real name was Sally. Little Nell's real name,

Darleen told me, was Laura. "Sally says her dad just picked the ugliest names he could think of to call his kids in the column."

Soon, Sally came to visit. She was as dazzling as Darleen, but in a wild, bohemian style, with huge looped earrings and tangles of untamed flame-red hair. I yearned for a fascinating friend like Sally—somebody different, who didn't live in a house just like ours and go to the same school and same church every Sunday. I thought about Nell, or Laura: how exciting to have an assumed name, an alias, a *nom de guerre,* or *de plume,* or *de* something. That was the kind of person I wished I could meet.

From my bedroom, I could hear Sally and Darleen laughing together over things too sophisticated for me to understand. Instead of getting on with my homework, I doodled in the margins of my notebook, over and over again, in different handwriting:

Nell/Laura
Nell=Laura
Nell Nell Nell.

My father was always writing songs and poems for people he admired—Einstein, Churchill. I decided to write one for Laura Campbell:

> *Now I know your name's not Nell*
> *It doesn't seem the same.*
> *But I still like you anyway,*
> *I know you're not to blame.*

When my father came in to say good night, I showed it to him. He laughed. "Why don't you send it to her?" He'd written fan letters to Ross Campbell over the years, and always received charming replies. In the morning, before I had a chance to change my mind, I asked Darleen for the Campbells' address and put the letter in the mail.

The reply lay in the yellow mailbox, buried under the bills and the supermarket fliers.

I put my school bag down on the hot concrete pathway and slit the envelope, and in that moment I found the opening I'd looked for to the wider world.

"I had a brainwave the other day, thinking you might like to be my pen-friend."

I held the letter as if the offer it contained was an admission to Harvard. "Actually," she wrote, "my name's not even Laura, it's Sonny."

I was enthralled. I wrote back immediately, trying hard to sound like someone worthy of a pen pal with three names.

Sonny wrote that she had another pen pal, a girl in Manchester, England. But that correspondent was about to be jettisoned. She had earned Sonny's disgust by expressing surprise that an Australian knew who the Rolling Stones were. "What does she think we are, kangaroos?" A Sydney pen pal mightn't be as exotic as an English one, but at least I wouldn't make gaffes like that. And the stamps would be cheaper.

Sonny lived just across town—ten miles as the crow flies. Her home was across the Harbour Bridge, on the side of the city known as the North Shore. Watery inlets and fingers of bushland full of bellbirds and cockatoos embraced its neighborhoods. Most homes there sprawled graciously on large lots set back from tree-lined avenues. In Sydney, North Shore signified affluence as surely as West End in London, or Beverly Hills in Los Angeles, although the wealth represented there was far less, and less ostentatiously displayed. From his columns, we knew that Ross Campbell took the train to work, worried about how to carve a single roast chicken into sufficient portions to feed family and guests, and resented the musical jingle of the ice cream truck because treats for his four children stretched his scarce cash supply. Like most Australians in the 1960s, Campbell, with his large family, portrayed himself as "an Aussie battler" striving to make ends meet. It was years before the rapacious decade of the 1980s would open up wide disparities of wealth.

Still, class existed, and announced itself in a dozen subtle ways. A North Shore family lived close enough to the best beaches to pop down for a dip, burdened by nothing more than a towel. For us, a trip to the beach meant driving over an hour through traffic. We went only on heat-wave days, when the temperatures became unbearable. My uncle would arrive in the pickup truck he used for his secondhand furniture business, and my cousin and I would ride in the back with the heavy paraphernalia—coolers, beach chairs, umbrellas—of those who have to "make a day of it." By early afternoon my skin, unaccustomed to beach glare, showed the first pink symptoms of the sunburn I'd carry home. It was in a series of such small distinctions that Australia's class lines were drawn.

But much more important than any geographic or class divide between Sonny and me was the difference in our ages. Sonny was just about to turn thirteen—making her more than two years older at an age when two years might as well be a yawning generation gap. At school, the idea of a sixth-grader approaching me, a humble fourth-grader, would have been as unlikely as a Brahmin consorting with an Untouchable. Somehow, pen-friendship magically erased these issues of caste and opened a window to Sonny's different world.

The extent of the difference was apparent in her second letter. Sonny Campbell didn't want to be a nurse or a teacher, and certainly not a nun. She would be, she informed me, "in Musical Comedy." What, she wanted to know, did I want to be?

This harmless question for her was a loaded one for me. I'd already learned that stating one's ambition could be a risky business.

. . .

"I wonder what it'd be like working at the hairdresser's," says Ann, peeling back the white bread of her sandwich to examine its contents.

It is lunchtime in the playground at St. Mary's. We cluster in the puddle of shade provided by the towering facade of the church. At the other end of the playground, high gates open onto the roar of Parramatta Road—six lanes of exhaust-belching cars, trucks and buses—the main artery westward from the city to the Blue Mountains and the endless Outback beyond. In between the road and the church is a treeless expanse of black asphalt marked up with a basketball court and rimmed with painted benches.

We sit in a little knot by the basketball hoop so we can talk to our friend Margaret, the team's goalie, as she shoots her prescribed one hundred daily practice goals. The rest of us unwrap the waxed paper contents in our Tupperware lunchboxes. The unlucky have sandwiches with Vegemite—a yeast-extract paste that looks like axle grease. The lucky have meat pies with dribbly brown gravy purchased at the "tuck shop" for one-and-a-penny (the equivalent of eleven cents).

"Hairdressing's a stinky job—all old ladies with blue rinses and perms," says Maureen, who wants to be a nurse. "You won't meet any boys."

"Well, the only people you'll meet'll have sores all over them or be chundering all the time. Imagine kissing someone after you've emptied their bedpan!" says Ann. We hoot at this, no one willing to raise the really awful part—that nurses see men's "privates," and even have to touch them.

"Dummies!" says Maureen. "Everyone knows nurses marry doctors, not patients."

"Why do you have to *marry* a doctor? Why not be one?" I

say. The others stare at me as if I've pulled a rotting fish from my lunchbox. Undaunted, I carry on. "I'm going to be a scientist. I haven't really decided the field yet, but most probably biochemistry." This doesn't seem out of the question to me. My mother has told me I can do anything. I believe her.

There is a hush first, as the others look at me, then at each other. Then they all explode in the raucous, untamed cackle of ten-year-olds.

I haven't yet learned that when you're in a hole you should stop digging. Flushed and hurt, I blurt out my retort: "All of you won't be laughing when you see the headline: 'Sydney Scientist Discovers Cure for Cancer.'"

To my fourth-grade classmates, I am hilariously out of line. Japanese have the saying that "the nail that sticks up gets hammered down." The Australian equivalent is the "tall poppy syndrome"—any Australian who rises above the crowd risks being cut down by a storm of derision. I have committed the cardinal sin of "having tickets on myself," or, more crudely, "being up myself"—an expression we use without knowing what it means.

Across the playground, the girls spot our teacher and run off to share the joke with her. This young nun is the best teacher the school has. In English class, she has set aside the tedium of parsing and analysis and allowed us to try our hand at writing our own poetry. Recently, she has begun introducing us to "nature study." These proto-science lessons are basic stuff to me—her chalk drawings of cells on the blackboard are a feeble reflection of the bright world I've explored through my microscope lens. I know the oozing form of the amoeba, the whimsical thrusts of its pseudopodia as it slinks across a slide. I've studied the matter of my own body; cells scraped from the inside of my cheek and the drop of blood squeezed from my finger. When she draws a simplified cell with nucleus and cell membrane, my hand shoots up. "Sister, you've left out the vacuoles and the plastids." My know-all demeanor must have driven her crazy. Whatever the reason, she joins in my classmates' laughter. I stand alone in the playground, my eyes stinging, my cheeks hot with the blush of humiliation.

After thinking about it, I decided that it would be safe to confide my goal to Sonny. At Sonny's school, no one made fun of ambition, or gave girls poor grades for art because of "bad types" in the art world. Most children in Sydney attended free government schools staffed by teachers well enough paid to make the career esteemed. My schoolteacher cousin was our family's most conspicuous material success, living in a big house with a pool, traveling abroad every other year. Catholics paid modest fees to attend our own schools, a little more disciplined, a little more personal than the government option.

And then there were a handful of schools like Sonny's: expensive and unabashedly elitist. Abbotsleigh was known for its excellence. Its alumnae, such as Jill Ker Conway, had made their marks in many fields, from traditional academics to avant-garde art. To announce that one wanted to be "in Musical Comedy" would have been certain social death at St. Mary's. But at Abbotsleigh it was a dream to be encouraged.

Like me, Sonny had missed a lot of school during a childhood illness. In her case, a bout of hepatitis when she was ten years old had kept her home for three months. She had spent her invalid days watching midday movies and had developed a taste for musical extravaganzas.

Her theatrical flair imbued every letter, turning the small businesses of childhood into high drama. She used punctuation decoratively, throwing in clusters of exclamation points like bouquets of flowers, to brighten things up. A trip down a stormwater drain became an epic trek to the heart of darkness: "We were half way through when a man threw a bucket of water down!!! It's pitch black the whole way but the good thing is, it's IMPOSSIBLE to get stuck, suphercate (or however you spell it) drown or anything else."

A week at camp was transfigured into a series of near-death experiences of perilous hikes and buses careening down mountains. "One day we hiked for MILES to the beach and when we got there, it was closed! We also hiked for miles to Church, but of course, it was open." Her world was full of experiences, ranging the streets in a clot of neighborhood kids, going to pajama parties—"boy! was it beaut! We talked ALL night (sorry, a bit of exajuration (or however you spell it) there we got to sleep at 1.30 AM!)."

Even her handwriting was dramatic, changing from cuneiform spikes in one letter to flamboyant curvaceous scrawls the next. "For my birthday," she wrote, "Sally gave me two divine garters. They're black lace with colored ribbon."

For my birthday, I got *The Student's Book of Basic Biology*— an illustrated tome I'd longed for. I racked my brains to make my letters as interesting as hers. My life had more to do with thinking than doing. It was solitary, full of books and the imaginary journeys they took me on. I had just discovered science fiction. I was devouring John Wyndham's *Day of the Triffids,* Ray Bradbury's *Fahrenheit 451* and C. S. Lewis's *Out of the Silent Planet* as fast as the library could order them. I spent more time than ever staring at the stars from the sun-warmed roof of the back veranda, imagining the unseen planets out by Alpha Centauri.

Sonny and I couldn't have been more different. But somehow we eked out a correspondence of equal parts dreams and dailiness. When she wrote to me excitedly that she was to make her television debut, I rushed home from school in time to see her, decked out in a cloud of tulle, dancing the role of White

Bird in an adaptation of an Aboriginal legend for an afternoon children's program. To me, it might as well have been a lead role in a Broadway hit. Sonny was on her way!

My progress toward my dream was more incremental. By then I was in better health and going to school regularly. My mother's one-on-one tutorials proved more than compensation for the months of classes I missed. I found that rather than being left behind I was embarrassingly ahead in all but mathematics, in which I continued to show a distressing lack of aptitude for a would-be scientist.

Sonny and I had one dream in common, and that was travel. It was the dream on which all the others depended. Sonny and I were members of the last generation of Australians who grew up knowing that one day we would have to go away. For those who had ambitions, Australia in the mid-1960s looked like a very small place. The Big Trip Elsewhere was a rite of passage and a test of nerve.

Sonny and I both knew the ritual of the International Terminal where the big white liners left for overseas. We had been to the docks to see off our sisters' friends, headed to England. The ships would carry hundreds at a time away from their country, and it seemed that thousands—the friends and families left behind—stood on the pier to say goodbye. We'd throw streamers to the travelers pressed against the railings of the departing ships. A riot of colored bands would loop from ship to shore, the travelers clutching one end, those remaining behind holding the other. Finally, the deep foghorn would groan and the ship would draw away. We sang "Auld Lang Syne" as the streamers pulled taut and finally snapped, wafting to rest for a moment, gaudy stripes on dark water, before the weight of the wet paper dragged them out of sight.

By then, the big ship would have disappeared, too, a patch of brightness passing through the Heads and away into the Pacific. It was the reverse of the First Fleet, the British ships carrying the outcasts no one wanted to the jail at the ends of the earth. In return, we sent back so many of our best—writers, scientists, actors, artists and entrepreneurs.

At the age of thirteen, Sonny already knew her destination would be London. To her, that was where culture came from, and where she would go to break into acting. At school, Gilbert and Sullivan operettas were the fodder for Abbotsleigh's annual school concerts. At home, she watched English TV dramas such as the *Forsyte Saga* and comedies such as *Not Only But Also*.

But I had already started looking in another direction. I wanted to go to America. I had known it from the midsummer evening in January 1961, when we gathered around our television set and watched a handsome young man with tousled hair being sworn in as President of the United States.

4

Beam Me Up, Joannie

"GLO-OORIA! Glory! Glor-eeeee!"

The voice over the back fence was as irritating as a buzz saw.

"Oh, for goodness' sakes, what does she want?" said my mother as she tilted my chin to the bright light that poured through the dining-room window. A smear of dust and blood started at my knees, blurred the front of my dress and smudged my split lip. It was a Saturday morning in 1963 and I'd just come off my backyard swing face first.

"GLORY! ARE YOU THERE? GLOR-EEEE!"

With a sigh of aggravation, my mother put down the wash-cloth and went out to see what her neighbor wanted. Edna, a lonely woman whose husband had deserted her, was always calling my mother for one trivial reason or another. Her voice carried through the screen door.

"Gloria, they've killed him. Someone's shot Kennedy."

Fresh tears stung my eyes and overflowed into the little runnels of dust down my cheeks. Australian Catholics loved

Kennedy; we considered him one of our own. My mother hurried back inside and switched on the radio.

Kennedy's election in 1960 turned Australia's gaze toward the United States. The new President's youthful glamor contrasted with our dreary old man Menzies who, by that time, had held power for eleven years. To lonely women like Edna, the conspicuously Catholic Kennedy was part saint, part pinup. Other Australians saw an idealism in him that resonated with their own sense of themselves as people of a young country. I was enthralled by a President prepared to imagine a place for human beings in space.

By the early 1960s even a sycophantic Anglophile like Menzies could see that Australia's future didn't lie entirely in its links to a tiny island across the world. Menzies saw an advantage in aligning himself with the popular American President. He listened to the urgings of Australia's chief diplomat in Washington, D.C., when he cabled that we could "without disproportionate expenditure pick up a lot of credit with the United States" by helping Kennedy in Vietnam.

My father's American-accented voice was one of the few raised against Australia's shift from British to American client state. "We don't need to get mixed up in a blue because of the Yanks," he said. (A "blue" is Australian slang for a fight.) "And we don't need Yank materialism shoved down our throats."

Most Australians saw nothing wrong with the new influences. We called Americans "Septics"—in rhyming slang, septic tank equals Yank. But there was no malice in the name. Americans, in most Australians' view, were a bit like golden retriever puppies—well-intentioned, good-humored, but a little thick. Many Australians had brushed up against them during World War II, when they took rest and recreation leave in Australian cities. There had been some blues over competition for women—the saying "Overpaid, oversexed and over here" reflected the view of the Aussie "Diggers," whose miserable army pay couldn't underwrite the free-spending good times the Americans showed their dates. But there were also lots of jokes about American ineptness, like the G.I. who showed up for a date with a lovely bunch of lantana—considered a noxious weed in Australia and most often seen covering country outhouses.

Slowly, American syndicated columnists began to leaven the British drone in our newspapers. In 1966 we shed the ridiculous complexity of the twelvepence-a-shilling, twenty-shillings-a-pound currency we'd inherited from Britain, and adopted a decimal system. While a few brave voices called for an indigenous Australian name for the new hundred-unit note, we settled for American-style dollars and cents. I walked around the house humming the jingle, sung to the tune of "Click Go the Shears," meant to prepare us for the change:

> *In come the dollars, in come the cents.*
> *Out go the pounds and the shillings and the pence.*
> *Be prepared, folks, when the coins begin to mix*
> *On the fourteenth of February 1966.*

"Just think," wrote Sonny excitedly, "tomorrow is 'change-over day' and I just saw my first 1 cent and 2 cent pieces." At school, the playground buzzed with excitement when someone scored one of the new coins. They may have been named for the United States currency, but their look was Australian, with interesting animals such as frill-necked lizards and platypuses on the obverse side. Unfortunately, the head on the other side remained the same boring old Brit, Elizabeth II.

On television American programs started to edge out British-made ones. It didn't seem odd to me to wander around humming the theme song to "Daniel Boone": ". . . and he fought for America to make all Americans free." Or to be able to recite the prologue to "Superman": "who . . . fights a never-ending battle for truth, justice, and the American way." On Tuesday nights, when my sister wanted to watch the British spy spoof "The Avengers," I lobbied desperately for the new American science-fiction series "Star Trek."

"Star Trek" arrived in Sydney in 1967, one year after its U.S. debut. From the first creaky pilot program where the aliens' makeup looked like it had been crafted hastily from Plasticine, I was hooked. I became obsessed with the starship *Enterprise* and its five-year mission to boldly go where no man had gone before.

For the first time in my life I had a non-nerdy interest I could share with others my age. I was about to turn thirteen, the age that robs so many girls of their childhood confidence. For me, the opposite happened. I had been shy and awkward before, and I would be again; but for a blissful couple of years I blossomed.

I was in sixth grade—the end of the line at St. Mary's. Soon our class would split up and go on to various regional high schools. But for the time being we were the "big girls" and we owned the playground. Before long I'd organized half of sixth grade into a parallel *Enterprise* crew, engrossed in a "Star Trek" game that we played every recess. Our group laid claim to a section of the playground benches, which became the *Enterprise* bridge. A popular classmate consented to play Captain Kirk. Soon the playground was ringing with commands: "Ahead warp factor one, Mr. Sulu. Open hailing frequencies, Uhura." When the "ship" hit a force field or came under fire from Klingons with the shields still down, we all fell about on the benches, simulating impact about as convincingly as the real cast on the set in Burbank. Our Dr. McCoy would crouch over the prone form of a classmate designated expendable, and intone: "He's dead, Jim," with perfect gravitas.

I played the half-Vulcan science officer, Mr. Spock. Actually, I *lived* Mr. Spock, cutting my bangs to match his basin-style haircut and surreptitiously plucking my eyebrows into as much of a slope as I could get away with. To convincingly imitate Mr. Spock's "That's illogical, Captain," I had to learn something about syllogisms and inductive versus deductive reasoning. I started borrowing textbooks on logic from the local library. Because innumeracy was undesirable in a science officer, I resolved to apply myself more diligently in math class. I sent away for a mail-order slide rule and instructions in how to use it. As a result, I mastered logarithms before I had a complete handle on long division.

In those days before tie-in merchandising, we improvised *Enterprise* paraphernalia, borrowing our fathers' electric shavers to stand in for "Beam me up, Scotty" communicators, and making Starfleet lapel pins out of cardboard and glitter. When a model kit for the *Enterprise* turned up at a local hobby shop, I braved the gaze of the boys buying Spitfires and biplanes, and for the next several days walked around slightly high from the airplane glue that seemed to adhere to everything but the flimsy plastic pieces of starship.

After school on Tuesdays, I fretted. I would hang around the phone, hoping Darleen would call to say she had a date for dinner and wouldn't be home in time for "The Avengers." Some afternoons, as the hour advanced, I'd actually be reduced to praying that someone would ask her out. I never told Darleen that divine intercession was responsible for the fact that she got so many dates on Tuesdays.

In December 1967 the cloned crew of the starship *Enterprise* said tearful farewells in the playground of St. Mary's and boldly went off to the strange new world of high school. I returned to Bland Street, to the school across the road from my parents' old Victorian terrace house.

At Bethlehem Ladies College, red brick classrooms and plasterboard temporary buildings jostled each other for space. The grounds were a treeless expanse of concrete and bitumen. But the headmistress was that rare thing in the 1960s: a feminist nun. Rather than arming us with facts and force-marching us by rote through the prescribed curriculum, Sister Ruth hired an eclectic staff encouraged to teach us how to learn.

A remnant of the old *Enterprise* crew had transferred to Bethlehem with me, but our desire to fall about on benches under Klingon attack withered under the gaze of the much older girls who shared the playground. Instead, we became avid consumers of "fanzines"—the badly printed, execrably written TV and movie magazines on sale at the railway station news-stand. I would devour the contents of these, then cut out every "Star Trek" picture for the growing collage on my bedroom wall. Soon the Sacred Heart was banished in favor of an enormous full-color picture of Mr. Spock, eyebrow raised quizzically.

It was in one of the fan magazines that I found the U.S. address for the Mr. Spock fan club. When its newsletter arrived, I was disappointed. I wanted to know about the planet Vulcan and the politics of the Federation and I couldn't care less about the family life or previous roles of an actor named Leonard Nimoy. But one feature in the newsletter caught my eye—a list of fan club members looking for pen pals.

Sonny had shown me that pen-friendship allowed the bridging of otherwise unbridgeable spaces. But I had failed to interest her in my "Star Trek" obsession. Sonny had obsessions of her own: the theater, tap class, ballet, singing lessons and, increasingly, boys. She planned to leave school as soon as she could, enroll in acting classes for a year, and then head for London. Slowly, our correspondence had worn down like an unwound clock.

A hot prospect in the fan-club newsletter was an American girl named Joannie who listed her interests as science and reading. She was just three months older than I. An American pen pal would see "Star Trek" episodes months before they were screened in Australia and would be able to fill me in on the plots. And she might be able to answer other questions as well. I was curious about the United States. I wanted to learn something about the world my father had inhabited when he was my age.

My father said very little about his California childhood. The few stories he did tell were so sad that I could hardly bear to listen. Slowly, I pieced together the outlines of his early life from stray remarks in adult conversations; things said and quickly hushed, hints dropped before the exchange of meaningful looks and brisk changes of subject.

My father's parents each had a wild streak. His mother, the daughter of an attorney, had been allowed to leave her home in New York's Saratoga Springs at the age of seven, to tour as cornet soloist with a band called the California Brownies. "Little Louise," as she was billed, developed an opium addiction and was married for the first time at sixteen. Soon after my father was born, the marriage ended when her husband caught her in bed with another man.

Lawrie's father was a doctor's son who split with his family to become a baseball player. He was a gifted athlete, a talented artist and a fine singer. He was also an alcoholic who would die young and indigent in a Salvation Army home.

Lawrie, six years old, was in the courthouse in Santa Barbara the day the judge in his parents' divorce case found both of them guilty of "moral turpitude." The judge awarded custody of the boy to his grandparents.

From sleeping on the veranda of his parents' tiny one-bedroom cottage, he found himself in a spacious house on the corner of Broadway and Main in Santa Maria. In those days, Santa Maria was a small farming town, but its tree-lined Broadway was a hundred feet wide, so that horse-drawn carriages could turn there.

I didn't bother to check an atlas before I wrote to Joannie. Otherwise, I might have learned that Maplewood, New Jersey, was a continent removed from my father's childhood haunts in Santa Maria, Pismo Beach and Fullerton.

Her first letter arrived in the yellow mailbox in late August 1968. It was plastered with stamps of Thomas Jefferson and the Statue of Liberty. In careful printing, Joannie wrote:

"I'd like to be your pen-pal. . . . I just turned 13 on June 4. . . . My favorite subject is, obviously, science (biology). . . . I, too, am crazy over L.N. My closet door is overflowing with pictures. The U.S.S. Enterprise, Jr. reposes on my bureau, and Mr. Spock, poster-size stares down from the wall! . . . Coincidence! I play recorder, too. . . . I'm an avid reader. I devour science, science fiction and fantasy. . . . Please write soon, and I'm glad that you're my new penpal." To my delight, she signed her letter with the Vulcan salutation, "Live long and prosper, Joannie."

Joannie, like me, was a late-life child of older parents. Her two brothers and one sister were in their twenties. I had a beloved dog and cat; Joannie had a menagerie—dog, cat, kittens, mice (named Mr. Spock, Desilu, Constellation, Eugene McCarthy and Leila), guinea pigs, even water snails. She wanted to be an astronomer. Clearly, that ambition didn't raise anybody's incredulous eyebrows, since her eldest brother was a molecular biologist at Stanford University.

"I'm having some photographs developed and if there's a good one I'll send you it next letter. If you want a general description though—I'm five feet three inches tall, weigh 98 lbs., hair dark blonde, eyes green-brown. Okay?"

It certainly was okay. Everything about Joannie was okay by me. We were so much alike, even down to our height and weight. When she sent me her yearbook picture, it revealed an oval-faced beauty with long, honey-colored hair and a black velvet choker around a swanlike neck.

We wrote to each other every week. Instead of a mundane date such as Dec. 13, Joannie would head her letters 6812.13—a pseudo-star date like the kind Captain Kirk used for the log entries that began each "Star Trek" episode. As I'd hoped, she gave me the rundown on upcoming adventures: "Here's another Star Trek: 'Plato's Step Children,' a study of power induced depravity. The power is psychokinesis (direct action of mind over matter). Its wielders are arrogant sadists who force visitors to inflict indignities on themselves. . . . First rate." (This episode contained TV's first ever interracial kiss, when the aliens forced Kirk and Uhura to smooch for their amusement.) In return, I filled Joannie in on the plots of episodes from the first season of the series, which had aired before she started watching the show.

When NBC threatened to cancel the program after only seventy-nine episodes, we were among the fans who deluged the network with protest letters. Joannie sent thirty-six. By then, she was signing off her letters not only with the Vulcan salutation, but actually writing it in Vulcan: *Lash doro V'Succa*.

In retrospect, it's easy to see why this program absorbed us, as it did so many others. At thirteen, we were beginning to wake up to the world, only to find it a tragic and perilous place. Girls in my class were seeing their older brothers go reluctantly to Vietnam. The help that Menzies had sent in order to ingratiate himself with Kennedy had burgeoned from a few trainers into a full-scale troop commitment, including conscription. Australia now had CIA spy satellite bases in the Outback that would make us a target in a nuclear war. Life seemed precarious, even in faraway Sydney. To Joannie, the chill of the Cold War was icy.

"Last night around eleven fifteen P.M. the whole sky lit up all over pale orange for a few seconds and then there came the loudest thunderclap I've ever heard," Joannie wrote. It was an oil refinery explosion, "but at the moment it happened I was sure that a Bomb had fallen. It was really scary because I was so sure of it that I was almost wondering to myself, 'How much longer am I going to be alive?' We could see the flames from our second floor. . . . Afterwards I realized that had it been a bomb I wouldn't have been alive, because the ones they have today are so powerful to destroy everything far beyond twenty miles from New York, which is appx. where we are."

In "Star Trek's" optimistic scenario, we had survived the twentieth century. The Cold War was over, because the Russian, Pavel Checkov—"Keptin! Keptin! The Klingon ship is wery close!"—was part of the *Enterprise* crew. Race didn't matter, because a black woman was communications officer. Humanity's face in the twenty-third century was a reassuringly benign one.

But Joannie and I had to live in 1968, and as the year drew to a close it was the day-to-day reality of our own times, rather than the weekly escapism of "Star Trek," that began to occupy our correspondence.

Joannie sent me a poster: "War is not healthy for children and other living things." I pinned it up over my desk and sent her an Australian Vietnam Moratorium button, a red badge with white Vs radiating from the center that had become the popular symbol of opposition to the war. I wrote passionately of my antiwar beliefs, and questioned her about her politics.

"Yes," she wrote back, "I am a Eugene J. McCarthy supporter. I was very disappointed that McCarthy wasn't nominated. Such a horrible choice—Nixon and Humphrey! America is deteriorating." Since this was also my father's view, I had no doubt it was correct.

My father had turned his back on America with the same finality with which he had ended his singing career. He viewed the country of his birth the way a parent views a child who has grown up to be a disappointment. Through his eyes, I saw the California of his childhood as a golden place, full of promise. But materialism and overdevelopment had ruined it. In Sydney, he saw the unspoiled Los Angeles of his youth. He despised the Darwinistic individualism of the United States. His views were a much more comfortable fit with the cooperative, collectivist spirit of the Aussies he'd met in the Outback, in the army, and at his job in the trade-union-dominated printing industry.

Ever since he quit singing in 1961 his life had been bracketed by a dreary, hourlong bus commute to an eight-to-four proofreading job. But he never seemed restless in his workaday routine. He loved the English language; he took grammar and spelling errors personally. He crusaded for the correct usage of words like "decimate" and "juggernaut." To say "centered around" rather than "centered on" was to invite a lecture. All through school, I felt torn about whether to give him my essays to proofread. I knew he would catch every error. On the other hand, his indelicately scrawled proofreader's hash marks would mean I had to make the effort of rewriting the paper.

I think he also felt contented in his job because the men he worked with at the newspaper were his ex-army buddies and fellow musicians—his mates. It's hard to convey the freight carried by that loaded Australian word. It signifies a singular, fierce friendship between man and man that doesn't seem to exist in quite the same form in any other country. Reams have been written about Aussie mateship: its origins in the cruelties of convict life when six of every seven prisoners were men; its tempering by the hardships of isolated Outback settlement; its parasitic effect on male-female intimacy; its tendency to promote a particularly vicious, defensive brand of homophobia. But I think that for my father it was mostly a good thing, a surrogate for all the different kinds of man-to-man relationships his own upbringing hadn't provided.

Although his grandmother was a kindly woman, the big house in Santa Maria was a lonely place for a little boy. Ronald, his only sibling, had died at fifteen months, when my father was just two weeks old. All his life, my father was tormented by the possibility that his arrival had caused his parents to neglect his brother's signs of illness. With his father gone, brother dead and grandfather austerely distant, his one friend was a large orange cat named Silver. There is a picture of my father, a sad-eyed little boy, clutching the cat, rubbing his face into its fur. Not long after the photo was taken, the cat fell into a rainwater barrel and drowned.

Over the years, his mother worked her way through a series of husbands that included card sharks and moonshiners. When he was allowed to visit, he learned that one way to avoid abuse from these men was to be quick when the police arrived. His job was to grab the lid of the still and make off with it into the woods. If the still wasn't intact, the police couldn't prove that moonshining was under way. No matter how awful each visit, at the end of it Lawrie would beg his mother to let him stay with her. She always turned him down.

If my mother formed my imagination, my father shaped my politics. Sometimes he would arrive home in midafternoon with an announcement that there was a blue at the paper. The dispute may have concerned the hourly rate paid to rural delivery men or an insult to a copy boy. But the Australian rule was "one out, all out," so the whole staff of the newspaper, from journalists to janitors, would be on strike until it was resolved.

Even though strikes meant lost wages, my father enjoyed these blues. He loved to see the workers flex their muscle in a good cause. And even if the cause wasn't so good, he loved to see the bosses squirm.

He had been militantly pro-union even as a singer, trying to organize the diverse egos of individualistic musicians. He worked on the headline performers, the stars, reminding them of the hard conditions they'd encountered on their way up, and warning that they'd meet them again on the way down, if the people in the spotlight didn't take a stand on behalf of the people in the chorus line. "You think your talent will protect you?" he'd argue. "Maybe it will while you're at the top of the bill, but who knows how long you'll be there."

In our family, it was a given that we always favored the battler over the silver-tail, the little bloke over the boss-cocky. Anyone who crossed a picket line was lower than a snake's armpit. And a scab—well, even my father's extensive and colorful vocabulary didn't have words for the degree of contempt in which such a person was held. To underline what we thought of scabs, he told me what had befallen one reporter who had stayed at work when his mates had a blue. On his way home from helping the bosses put out the strike paper, the tram conducter had refused to sell this scab a ticket. Worse, his local pub wouldn't serve him a beer, and even the night-soil carters of those pre-sewer days refused to empty his outhouse bucket. This, according to my father, was the worker solidarity that made Australia great.

My father despised Menzies's misnamed Liberal Party, which was conservative, probusiness and antiunion. He always voted for the Labor Party—which meant he'd voted for losers in every election since 1949. An election, for him, was just like any other blue, and in any blue he always backed the underdog.

That rule applied even if the blue happened to be a millennial conflict taking place half a world away. My father always had an opinion; he always knew exactly where he stood. And, desperate to find some common ground with this puzzle of a parent, I scrambled to find a way to stand there with him.

5

Shalom, Mate

꧁꧂

"Daddy, can I have a stamp?"

"Oh, nuts! Hell's bells! Why doesn't your mother ever buy stamps?"

My father has a clutch of these archaic semicurses. Asking to borrow something always elicits one. Profligate and reckless with household finances, my father is meticulous about his own small horde of possessions. He always has an ample supply of stamps and aerograms in his bedside drawer, so that if he feels a midnight urge to dash off a letter to the Prime Minister of the United Kingdom or the director of the local sewage authority, he will be able to do it.

He gives me the stamp; he always does. And then, when I tell him what it is for, he even looks pleased to have helped me. I skip away and post a letter to a pen pal in Israel.

. . .

Of an evening, our dog would hear my father's tread on the front steps before a figure appeared fuzzily through the ripple-glass door.

Timing was everything. If the dog ran to the door by six or a little after, the evening would be uneventful. Any time after six-thirty, things got iffy. My mother, making dinner in the kitchen, would glance at the dining-room clock, dry her hands on a tea towel and go to greet him. No matter what came after, they always hugged like newlyweds.

You could tell how it would be by his mouth. Usually it was an amiable mouth, turned up at the corners, ready to smile at the dog, greet the cat and enjoy a quiet evening in front of the television or in bed with a book. On nights he was late, it would be another man's mouth; a mean, thin line attached to a bellowing, unreasonable stranger who would pick a fight over a piece of lint on the floor or the position of the soap dish.

We learned to give this metamorphosed man a wide berth, which is one reason we had abandoned attempts at a family dinner. With plates propped on our laps in front of the TV, it was possible that the outbursts of irrational anger would be directed at a politician on the nightly news, or a grammatical lapse in a sit-com script.

One Tuesday evening I'd settled down to enjoy the weekly episode of "Star Trek." I had already completed the obsessive-compulsive routines necessary to savor this, my favorite hour of the week. To better assimilate every detail of the plot, I positioned myself on the floor, three feet from the screen, cushions propped, pad and pen beside me to jot down notes during commercial breaks. William Shatner's sonorous voice had no sooner intoned the familiar "Space. The final frontier" than my father erupted from his armchair.

"It isn't, you know! What about the human brain! We're only using one percent of the brain's capacity—that's the final bloody frontier! Hell's bells, who writes this garbage?" His voice, his wonderfully trained singer's voice that could fill an auditorium, boomed like a cannon in our living room. "Stop yelling," my mother said. "I'M NOT YELLING!" he yelled. On he went, and on, about the intellectual deficiencies of Hollywood script writers, the narrowness of the cultural debate, our inferior moral fiber for supporting such drivel by watching it.

There was no way to short-circuit one of these diatribes. To interrupt was simply to refocus his anger on oneself. By the day after, he would have forgotten everything he'd said. The positive side to his amnesia was that it taught us not to take his abuse to heart. The negative side was that the whole argument could be rerun dozens of times, often word for word. That was how it was with the "Star Trek" introduction. If my father had been drinking, the words "The final frontier" would be like the bell to Pavlov's dog. He would thunder, "It isn't, you know!" And off he would go again on his tirade. Eventually, we made a joke out of it, competing to see who could be quickest to get out the words "It isn't, you know." My father would look at us with a puzzled expression, murmur, "Too bloody right," and wander off to find a mis-hung tea towel to complain about.

These alcohol-induced tempers were the unscourable residue of my father's earlier self, a small untidy corner in what had become an otherwise orderly life. One or two of them were the blight on each otherwise tranquil week.

But for six days in June 1967, the belligerent stranger didn't appear at the door at all. Instead, my father arrived home early every night, anxious to catch the headlines on the six o'clock news. Afterward, he spread the evening papers on his bed and pored over the maps inside. Tiny Israel was at war, and he cared passionately.

That meant I cared too. Unlike my mother, who could enter

a child's world with ease and spend comfortable hours there, my father could only deal with us as miniature adults. His strange, sad childhood had left him with no detailed pattern of father-hood to follow. I learned that if I wanted to talk to him it was easier to follow his adult interests wherever they might lead. Sometimes it was the shade of a sprawling fig tree by the cricket pitch where he managed the local under-sixteen team. Gritting my teeth to keep from yawning through the interminable games, I learned to mark the score card and toss off phrases like "caught at deep fine leg" and "bowled a maiden over."

Those odd, colorful expressions were all I really liked about the game. I hated sports. Being sick for so long had left me unathletic and poorly coordinated. All through primary school I was the second slowest runner in every race, able to beat only the little girl in my class who had Down syndrome.

So, when my father's attention wandered from the crease at the cricket ground to a volcanic plateau called the Golan Heights, I was only too happy to follow him there.

He was a convert to the Zionist dream. Serving in Palestine in World War II, the socialist in him had fallen in love with the idea of the kibbutz. His California family, transplanted East Coast WASPs named Ithamar and Winthrop, with roots going back to the American Revolutionary War, had been garden-variety anti-Semites. His own experience in Hollywood had ex-posed him to all the conspiracy theories of Jews controlling press, pictures, radio and finance. But the unexamined preju-dices with which he grew up couldn't long survive his en-counters with the swamp-draining, poverty-embracing Jewish pioneers. These Jews were underdogs, and my father naturally gravitated to their cause.

"What did we see in Palestine?" he wrote in a wartime letter to an Australian friend. "We saw acres of barren, badly culti-vated land, suddenly studded with some glorious green oasis rife with all manner of growing things, a jewel of productiveness in the midst of a wasteland. This would be a Jewish community farm, inhabited by Jews from every part of the world, living, working together happily, harmoniously; generous and friendly to outsiders, and in very few ways resembling the palm-rubbing, money-grubbing, successful Jew we know and so often despise in our own setting."

During that week in 1967, I peered over his shoulder at the newspaper maps as he traced the progress of the fighting for me, describing the geography of the Sinai Peninsula and the Jordan Valley. It was the first time I had paid attention to anything in the newspapers beyond the comics. For six days my head was full of the kibbutznik children huddled in shelters as the Syrian mortars rained down. When Israel won, we celebrated.

From then on, I read Leon Uris and Anne Frank, learned Yevtushenko's "Babi Yar" by heart and ostentatiously hauled around a dog-eared copy of *The Rise and Fall of the Third Reich.* Eventually I took to wearing a Star of David to school, much to the consternation of the nuns.

With the same intensity I had expended on becoming Mr. Spock and recreating the bridge of the *Enterprise* in the school playground, I decided I would become a Jew and move to Israel. To practice for my new life on the kibbutz, I cultivated my mother's modest vegetable garden to the point of soil erosion and designed an ambitious tree-planting campaign to drain our desiccated backyard's nonexistent swamp.

One problem in my scheme seemed insurmountable, though. I had never met a Jew. I had hoped that Joannie might be Jewish, but when I wrote to her about my growing Israel obsession, her reply had been disappointing. "I have read both 'Mila 18' and 'Exodus'. I enjoyed (if that's the word) them both, even though my last year's history teacher insists that if anyone can't write it's Leon Uris. As for support of either Arab or Israelis, I suppose that I support Israel, although there's right and wrong on both sides. I don't have any allegiance to Israel because I'm not Jewish, but many of my friends who are consider Israel rather than the USA to be their true homeland. I don't really blame them; I'd rather be almost anything than an American. . . ."

Right and wrong on both sides! Stunned by my pen pal's victimization by Arab propaganda, I scrawled a long, boring reply setting out the Zionist case. How could her Jewish friends have left her laboring under such a misapprehension? But at least Joannie had some Jewish friends. My prospects for finding any seemed dim. Sydney's small Jewish community had settled far away in the affluent eastern suburbs, where Mitteleuropean matrons gathered at coffee shops to nibble Sacher torte and talk about opera. Our western suburbs neighbors were still overwhelmingly of my mother's Irish stock—hard-worked housewives who relaxed over a "cuppa" at the neighbors' or gathered at the local Returned Services League club (the Australian version of the American Legion) for a flutter on the poker machines or the Wednesday afternoon races.

At school we had increasing numbers of immigrants—Italians, Poles, Lithuanians—but all of them were Catholic. Two of my best friends' families were from the Middle East—Zita's from Lebanon and Angela's from Alexandria, Egypt. Another classmate, Monique, was a Palestinian whose father's village was destroyed by Israelis after the 1948 Israeli War of Independence. Monique spoke Arabic and French before she'd learned English. Working in her third language, she was no match for me in history-class arguments. I remember her eyes, filled with tears, as she sat down in frustration after I'd delivered a passionate oration rebutting her account of her family's forced flight at the hands of the Jewish fighters.

Zita and Angela were easier converts to my point of view. The two of them helped me write and perform a one-act Holocaust play for English class. (SCENE: WARSAW GHETTO 1942. A DIMLY LIT CELLAR.) They played Ruth and Eva, two Jewish sisters hiding from Nazis. The centerpiece was a long monologue by Ruth, ostensibly read from her diary, cataloguing Nazi crimes against Jews in Poland, including the horrors of a death camp identified in the script as Austwich.

Speech delivered, Ruth becomes expendable. Two Nazis break into the cellar. (We enlisted a Lithuanian classmate who had the right tall blond looks for one of these parts; for the other we had to make do with an Italian.) The first Nazi, Helmet Fitzbrak, summarily executes Ruth. The other Nazi berates him: "You mad man—you ruined our sport. The men would have loved her." Eva then swallows a cyanide pill.

At this point I make my entrance as the girls' brother Baraak, a brave resistance fighter. Baraak shoots Helmet, stabs Wilfred. Alone on the corpse-strewn stage, he delivers a stirring monologue to the effect that resistance is the secret of joy. (CURTAIN).

Incredibly, this was well received by our English teacher, and we got an excellent mark for it. Emboldened, I asked her to add Leon Uris to the class reading list. When she explained that she thought his books were execrably written propaganda, I was completely baffled by her sudden failure of discernment.

I decided that there was only one way around the lack of Jews in my circumscribed orbit: I would have to find an Israeli pen pal. It seemed unlikely that I would find such a person in the Spock fan-club newsletter. Israelis were surely too busy tilling the soil and fighting guerrillas to watch TV. I imagined them huddled around crackly radios, listening to the news and an occasional Holocaust documentary.

I was considering writing to the Israeli Embassy in Canberra when I noticed a small advertisement in the children's pages of the Sydney newspaper for the International Youth Service, an organization a world away, in Finland, that arranged pen-pal correspondences. For a small fee, they would pair Australians with would-be correspondents elsewhere in the world.

Obviously, my plan called for my correspondent to be a boy, so I could eventually marry him. For the same reason, he needed to be at least a year older than I. Listing these requirements in my request to Finland's International Youth Service, I pondered what to write under "interests." I put down "Zionism, agriculture" and then, to make myself sound a little broader, since I had read that kibbutzniks valued learning and culture as well as the skills of farmer and warrior, I added "science, art, reading, flute and pets." I mulled the inclusion of "pets" for a while before opting for honesty over strategy. I hoped that my Israeli—no doubt laboring long hours in the cow sheds and turkey coops—wouldn't think pets were too bourgeois.

After a long wait, the reply finally came. I returned home from school to find it sitting in the silver dish on the side table where my mother put the sorted mail. She took care of the bills. What was left, most days, were the letters in answer to my father's eclectic correspondence. But since I'd started writing to Sonny and Joannie, often there would also be a letter in the dish for me.

The Hebrew postmark and the stamp picturing Jerusalem's Jaffa gate thrilled me. His name was Mishal, and as I tore the letter open, I was prepared to fall in love with my young sabra correspondent, right there where I stood on the pale green carpet of our dining room.

From the first paragraph, the letter was a litany of tiny disappointments. Mishal wrote that he didn't live on a kibbutz. However, it could have been worse; he wrote that he had worked on one "in the summer for a few days."

It seemed that Mishal's family wasn't exactly pioneer stock. His father, rather than draining the Hula Swamp, worked as a French-polisher. Somehow, French-polished furniture hadn't figured in my mental image of Israeli interiors. Hand-hewn cypress logs propped on spent shell casings was more the kind of décor I'd pictured.

But the worst blow of all came in paragraph four, where Mishal listed the languages he knew. "I also know Arabic, because I am an Arabian fellow."

Yech. I stuffed the letter back in its envelope, picked up my school case and trudged dejectedly to my room. It hadn't occurred to me that in asking for an Israeli pen pal I might get a reply from an Israeli Arab—a descendant of one of the 156,000 Arabs who had stayed and not fled during the 1948 war, and so became Israeli citizens. I needed an Arab boy for a pen pal like I needed an outbreak of acne. I wasn't too impressed by the males in my Arab girlfriends' families. Their brothers seemed spoiled to me. And I preferred my own father's benign detachment to the stifling presence of their fathers, always hovering and anxious, outside the most staid of parties or school functions.

When my father talked of the Arabs he'd met in the Middle East, it was mainly as figures of fun. His imitation of an Egyptian pimp's sales pitch—"Nice girls, very cleeeen, very hygieeeen"—was delivered with the stooped, cringing posture that is a classic of the better-recognized brand of anti-Semitism. He had taught me some Arabic he picked up in Egypt: I knew how to say *"Ana miskeen* [I'm poor]" when I wanted to weasel out of paying for something, and *"Malesh* [It doesn't matter]" when I'd botched a task or made a mess.

Leon Uris's prose on the subject, meanwhile, took ethnic slurs to lofty heights. Mishal lived in Nazareth, a place described in some detail in *Exodus* when the Zionist hero Ari Ben Canaan takes the American nurse, Kitty Fremont, on a road trip:

> They drove through the timeless Arab villages into the fertile carpet of the Jezreel Valley, which the Jews had turned from swamp into the finest farmland in the Middle East. As the road wound out of the Jezreel towards Nazareth again they moved

backwards in time. On one side of the hill the lush lands of the Jezreel and on the other, the sun-baked, dried-out, barren fields of the Arabs. . . . Nazareth stank. The streets were littered with dung and blind beggars made wretched noises and barefoot, ragged, filthy children were underfoot. Flies were everywhere. Kitty held Ari's arm tightly as they wound through the bazaar and to a place alleged to be Mary's kitchen and Joseph's carpenter shop.

Kitty was baffled as they drove from Nazareth: it was a dreadful place.

"At least the Arabs are friendly," Ari said. "They are Christians."

"They are Christians who need a bath."

I didn't think any of this would be much help in constructing an appropriate reply to Mishal: "Had any baths lately? I hear you have a lot of dung in Nazareth." Still, there had to be a reply; pen-pal etiquette demanded it. This went beyond manners into the realm of superstition. To fail to answer a pen-pal letter was to invite the same dose of bad luck as walking under a ladder or opening an umbrella indoors. The only way out of an unwanted correspondence was to keep replies cool, dull and brief, and to delay sending them in the hope that in the long interregnum the other party would lose interest. I crafted something suitable, and let it sit on my desk for weeks.

Meanwhile, I wrote away again to the pen-pal service, asking for another Israeli. I resisted the impulse to scrawl "Send me a goddamn Jew!" across my application. Instead, to make myself perfectly clear, I added "Judaism" to my list of interests.

Mishal's next letter arrived in no time. Undaunted by my brief note, he'd responded with a lengthy three and a half closely written pages. This was almost unheard of in the early stages of pen-friendship, especially from a correspondent writing in his third language. (Like all Israeli Arabs, Mishal was fluent in

Hebrew as well as Arabic.) Also, he'd enclosed a one-shekel coin, which thrilled me, and a postcard of the Cathedral of the Annunciation, which looked depressingly like St. Mary's Concord. Mishal wrote of Nazareth's pilgrims and ancient churches. Living in a Jewish state and on top of a Christian pilgrimage site made religion a defining part of his life.

My father's stubborn failure to convert to Catholicism had hastened the unraveling of my own faith. As time passed and no conversion appeared to be in the offing, it came to seem extremely unfair to me that a decent bloke like Daddy was doomed to eternal torment. By the time I reached high school, I'd just about had it with the arrogant local priests who were so sure about who God had time for. Darleen, my role model in all matters, had already begun to have Doubts.

When Pope Paul issued the encyclical banning birth control, it was my *casus belli*. I leaped to my feet in religion class and delivered myself of a Martin Lutheresque denunciation of the Church. A wise and humorous woman named Sister Gabriella taught the class. She also coached me in the debating team, and had befriended me in a way I'd never expected from a teacher, much less a nun. She handled my apostasy as she did a poorly prepared debate speech, astutely critiquing the flaws in the development of my argument and pointing out obvious openings for rebuttal. Then, to my surprise, she moved smoothly on with the day's class topic, the Catholic concept of reincarnation, as if the whole edifice of Rome hadn't just been shaken to its foundations.

Mishal lived in a place where religion couldn't be given away like an outgrown suit. In Israel, to be a Jew, a Christian or a Muslim permanently defined both status and prospects. As a Christian, he was part of the majority in Nazareth, but he became a minority every time he left the city.

Yet he seemed at home in the Jewish state. Despite his shaky grammar, he wrote of the beauty of Jerusalem's Old City, the constant flow of pilgrims in Nazareth, the modern vitality of Tel Aviv. "I know that you like the life in the kibbutz, and indeed the life in the kibbutz is very nice. There are a big hall to eat in and it is like the socialist life. Everyone works on the farm and in the fields." He added glimpses of his own life—his flute and guitar lessons, his large family—"I have five brothers and one sister. The number of sisters is equal in our families." He seemed genuinely curious about my life in Sydney, and as I sat down to reply, I found my resolution to shed him as a correspondent weakening.

"Is there Arabs in Australia? And did you know some of them?" he asked. You bet, I wrote, proudly telling him about my girlfriends. As I wrote about making stuffed vine leaves at Zita's house, the spicy smells of her mother's kitchen flooded back to me. I'd enjoyed being part of her boisterous extended family and the female food-assembly line of aunt, grandmother, mother and sisters. I loved it when her grandmother, who spoke little English, covered my hands with her work-worn, callused ones, showing me how to shape the rice and tuck the leaves, all the time burbling encouragement in gentle Levantine Arabic. I wrote of their tiny but productive garden, its neatly staked tomato plants and grape arbor groaning with fruit. Before I knew it, I'd filled several pages myself.

Eventually, the pen-pal service sent me another name. The tiny slip read: E boy 7/54, meaning an English-speaking male whose July birthday in 1954 made him an ideal fourteen months older than I. But the really good news came on the next line, with the surname. Cohen!

Even I, who a decade later would fall in love with a man named Horwitz without realizing he was Jewish, recognized Cohen as an unmistakably Jewish name. But then I knew why I recognized it, and my heart sank. Somewhere in my obsessive reading, I'd discovered that the *cohains*—the priestly class of ancient Israel—weren't allowed to marry converts. My plan had gone awry again.

Within a couple of pale mauve aerograms, it became clear that my correspondent's priestly status wasn't the only impediment to a romance. Cohen was a Jew; Israeli-born, he was even a genuine sabra. But he was also dull. A dull Israeli, just like an Arab Israeli, was a possibility that hadn't occurred to me.

His brief letters were full of football, basketball and the beach—the same dreary subjects that obsessed the Aussie youths to whom I wouldn't give the time of day. All he knew about Sydney was that the Israeli soccer team had recently played there, and all he wanted to know about me was whether I'd seen the game. Actually, if I'd known, I might well have persuaded my father to take me, in the hope of meeting some Jews. But I still hated sports. I resented the way the Australian sports obsession sapped attention from intellectual achievement. I associated sports with the beer-puking louts who spilled out of the local pub after the games finished on Saturdays, making the footpath into a gantlet to be run by any women who wanted to pass.

It proved difficult to engage Cohen on anything else. He was almost sixteen—just two years from compulsory army service, but my questions on his feelings about this, the kind of unit he would apply for, his vision of life afterward, were lost either in his unwillingness to discuss big issues or his inability to frame adequate responses in his limited English.

A year later, I was surprised to find myself writing a Christmas card to Mishal. But when I thought of sending Cohen a Hanukkah wish, I realized it had been months since we'd last corresponded.

6

French Letters

I was four when I first heard French.

My mother and I were at the railway station on a chilly winter's day. She had bundled me up in red tights and a matching red corduroy hood that tied in a bow under my chin. I remember a handsome woman leaning down to me and smiling, saying something I didn't understand. She was complimenting me on my beautiful *chapeau*. My mother latched onto the word and carried it home with us. In the garden, she devised a game named Shop de Chapeau. A large crimson leaf was a flamboyant Easter bonnet, a small sepia and gold one a sophisticated pillbox hat. Packed in old shoeboxes and stacked on tree-branch shelves, they became the stock of the store's proprietress, Mademoiselle Poohbarre.

"But Madame looks *très chic* in ze green beret!"

"No, I think I prefer something with a brim."

"Well, in that case, may I show Madame the maroon felt?" I presented my mother with a shoe box containing a fallen camphor-laurel leaf. *"Oh là là! Magnifique, non?"*

My mother had never had a chance to learn French, but she loved the sound of the language. We augmented our vocabulary from the television: Maurice Chevalier midday movies, Morticia and her besotted husband Gomez in "The Addams Family" and Pepe-le-Pew, the amorous French skunk in the Disney cartoons.

I longed to learn French before I knew where France was. I yearned for high school, when foreign-language classes would begin. I was sure that acquiring another language would allow me to break the code of all those older and better cultures that I imagined elsewhere.

If I had opened my ears, I might have realized that I could have learned any number of languages just by listening to the neighbors.

While I was so busy writing away in search of foreigners, the world was arriving on my street. Every time a FOR SALE sign sprouted in a front yard, my mother's friends—Edna and the other Irish Catholic "old-timers"—would gather to gossip over cups of tea and wonder apprehensively whether the place would be bought by "New Australians." Almost always, it was. Soon we were surrounded: we had a Turk over the back fence, Serbs next door, Greeks across the road, Italians, Russians, Lebanese and Chinese in the next block.

I was too young to give the changes much thought. But to people of Edna's generation the sudden diversity was shocking in a country built on racist exclusion. Migrants were supposed to be British, or Europeans who could pass for British. Australia feared Jews, blacks and especially the "Yellow Peril" from nearby Asia. For years, the nation's best weekly magazine, the *Bulletin,* had carried the slogan "Australia for the White Man" under its masthead. The atmosphere had been so racist that the immigration minister, Arthur Caldwell, could summarize his opposition to Asian migrants with quips such as "Two Wongs don't make a white."

The exclusion was enforced by a "dictation test" administered to any nonwhite migrant who somehow made it to Australia's shores. The test wasn't, as might seem likely, to measure a would-be migrant's proficiency in English. If the immigration officer didn't think the migrants looked white enough, the test could be administered in Gaelic, Latin or Icelandic—any language that would doom them to failure and deportation.

But by wartime there weren't enough British or Irish migrants to satisfy the labor needs of the growing country, and so a few more exotic people began to slip through the net. Immigration officers were told to select those who were "sixty percent European in appearance and outlook"—whatever that meant.

We called these first non-Anglo-Celtic migrants "Balts" no matter where in northern or eastern Europe they actually came from. Blond, blue-eyed, they were easy enough to get used to, once one got over the annoyance of their funny accents. The "Eye-Ties"—the large wave of Italians, Greeks and other southern European immigrants that followed the Balts—were more conspicuous with their dark complexions and pungent foods, and were met with more racism. It wasn't until 1965 that the "White Australia" policy was abandoned. Most Australians came to accept, sometimes grudgingly, that diversity was actually making the place more interesting. Now, racism expresses itself in debates over the number of immigrants wanted, rather than what color they should be.

My mother embraced the newcomers much sooner than the rest of the neighbors did. She befriended the lonely migrant women and worked on their English, and when she found they were being ripped off doing piecework for a pittance, she helped them use Australian labor laws to get a fairer deal. She became the children's advocate in their inevitable clashes between the ways of the adopted country and the abandoned one. When the Greek across the road lost his job at a car plant because his flight home from a family funeral had been delayed a day, my mother got on the phone and badgered the foreman into rehiring him. When the bachelor who lived over the back fence talked of returning to Turkey to find a suitable bride, my mother tried to figure ways to introduce him to "a nice Australian girl."

I loved the new world that these people opened up for me: the decadence of being offered a tiny glass of slivovitz by the Serbs on Sunday mornings, the gothic grieving of the Greeks when a distant cousin died, sipping tea in ornate cups from the Russian spinster's samovar, the strong tastes of black beans and chili oil brought by the Chinese and the arias that would burst unexpectedly from the Italian.

And yet the fact that they had come to Australia devalued them in my eyes. Why would anyone leave Rome or Athens or Beirut or Leningrad? Italy had scary terrorists, Greeks had military dictatorships, the Middle East had wars, the Russians had brave dissidents. To me, the banal certainty of three meals on the table, a steady job and stable politics seemed a pallid swap. My pen pals were still out there, amid the danger and the culture. So it was to them that I continued to look for my lifeline to the world.

The culture I particularly envied was French. One dull Sunday afternoon Darleen swooped down and swept me off to a Rodin exhibition at the Art Gallery of New South Wales. It was the first art I had ever seen up close. I gazed at Rodin's desperately heroic *Burghers of Calais,* his towering *Balzac,* his delicately entwined *Lovers.*

From Rodin, I moved on to the Impressionists, the Surrealists, the Dadaists, the Fauves. It was easy to love Cézanne's landscapes because they so much resembled our own. His clear Provençal light might have been Sydney light; his rock-ribbed hillsides differed only in their extra centuries subdued to the hand of man. At the time, I didn't realize I loved these paintings because they were showing me a way to look at my own country. I thought I loved them because they showed me a country that was better than mine.

There was a name for this syndrome: Cultural Cringe—the Australian belief that just about anybody anywhere did things better than we did. And no wonder. It was always other people and places we saw reflected in books and movies, never ourselves. I was seventeen before a major Australian novel (Patrick White's *The Tree of Man*) elbowed its way onto one of my classroom reading lists. In history, we spent weeks studying the U.S. Civil War, but no time at all on the Australian miners' rebellion against British troops at the Eureka Stockade. Australians still made few films. Our painters still often used misty European hues rather than the stark palette dictated by Australia's own crisp light and air.

We didn't even recognize the gifts of our native plants. One of my chores was sweeping up the pesky brown detritus that fell into our yard from a neighbor's tree. I didn't know that the Minié balls I was consigning to the compost were macadamias. These delicious nuts didn't become famous until an American exported seedlings to Hawaii.

With materials borrowed from Darleen, I began painting. Slowly my palette, easel and pieces of primed Masonite began to take over the space on the back veranda that my science lab had occupied. Instead of copper sulfate solution, dribbles of acrylic paint began to threaten the contents of my mother's ironing basket.

My artistic inspirations were all French. If Israel represented my craving for risk and adventure, it was France that made me hunger for a culture that was old and arrogant, serene in its own superiority.

In 1968, I finally began to study French at high school. For someone of my temperament, it was an auspicious year to start. I had developed the bad habit of doing my homework sprawled in front of the television set. As I struggled to devise sentences using the irregular verbs "to be" and "to have" the TV news offered a brief film clip from Paris. The street seemed to be on fire. In the midst of the flames, a devastatingly handsome Parisian student ripped up a cobblestone and hurled it at the police. It was May 1968, and the *événements* were under way.

"*Il est un beau étudiant,*" I wrote. "*Il est en fureur. Il a colère.*" *Et moi,* I thought, *j'ai colère aussi.* I wanted to hurl cobblestones, too—or I thought I did. I wanted to hurl something. I tingled all over with vague, nameless passions and urges. I wanted trouble, desperately. I wanted to kiss boys, take drugs, be hauled by the hair into a police van at an antiwar protest.

My parents were just as desperate to ensure that I did none of the above. For the next four years the tiny word "No" loomed large in Concord. No, I couldn't go on a date. No, I couldn't go to the beach with my girlfriends. No, I most certainly could not go and scream "Baby killer" at LBJ when he visited Australia.

Of course, I obeyed. Adolescent rebellion is problematic when your parents are your friends. But I ranted, I cried. I would have locked myself in the bathroom except that, since we only had one bathroom, locking oneself in it for any length of time seemed thoughtless. So I flounced through the house, singing loud, tuneless renditions of every song I knew with the word "free" in it: "Born Free," "I Want to Be Free," "Set Me Free, Why Don't You, Babe?" I blasted the "come mothers and fathers" verse from the "Times They Are A-Changing" at maximum volume, knowing that Bob Dylan's spectacular lack of vocal ability drove my father to distraction. I sulked in my bedroom over copies of *Rules for Radicals* and *The Electric Kool-Aid Acid Test*. My parents ignored it all, and in between outbursts we continued to get on famously.

Darleen, who could have been my advocate, was suddenly gone. Lured to Melbourne by a job as an advertising copy writer, she was now earning the phenomenal salary of a hundred dollars a week—almost twice what my father made. I moved into her room and hoped that the vibrations emanating from her décor—hessian drapes appliquéd with hippie-esque daisies, interesting junkyard-salvage bookshelves, rice-paper lanterns—would work some kind of transformation on my style-impaired psyche.

From Melbourne, Darleen became another pen pal. Her first letter arrived doodled all over like an illuminated manuscript with inks she'd purloined from the ad agency's art department. She had nicknamed me Face, gently mocking my discovery of heavy black eyeliner. "Heard you moved swiftly—up with the posters, on with the records—the dragon is dead—long live the face. How do you like the bed—bet you're getting good sleeps—well that's good—no lines for the face—right?"

From a distance, we drew closer. The letters got longer and more intimate. She sent me poems (Exley, Eliot), book recommendations (Tolkien, Vonnegut) and advice about boys: "With no brothers I found it hard to be natural at the beginning of my courting days." One day a letter arrived sharing sisterly confidences about work and romance. In it, she predicted our future: "We'll have little houses in Glebe and/or a dome house in the country, and we'll wizz around, drink lots of tea with mum, pick dad up from the races and cricket. And I'll either have a dog and lots of babies or a briefcase in the back seat and you'll have lots of impressionable young owl-eyed boy students five years your junior from your English classes at uni." She ended this letter with the words I'd longed for all my life: "And do you realise what an incredibly wonderful amazing thing it is to me to find I have a sister who has all the qualities, and more, that I look for in a friend. Much happiness, thank you face."

Worried that my curiosity about drugs would lead me into the company of creeps, she sent me a Glad sandwich bag containing a tiny amount of pot, also scored from her agency's art department. (No doubt from the "bad types" from whom the nuns of Concord had hoped to shield her.) I waited till Mum went down the street on a grocery errand, rolled a flaccid, emaciated joint, stood at the door of the back veranda and smoked it, fast. The spasm of coughing that followed was so intense that the dog started barking in sympathy. The back fence didn't melt. The magpies didn't start singing in harmonics. I didn't see God. Disappointed, yet ever the optimist, I fished a couple of seeds out of the crease in the bag and shoved them into the loamy soil among the begonias.

I decided that if I was to be imprisoned by the bourgeois values of my backwater country, at least I could write to some brave French soul out there on the ramparts. I had visions of her, my French alter ego. She wore tiny black mini-skirts and lashings of eyeliner. She chose her lovers with discernment. I visualized her hurling cobblestones by day and retreating to an intimate Left Bank brasserie where she argued about Simone and Sartre as the blended smoke of Gauloises and marijuana thickened in the candlelight. I decided to ask my French teacher to help me find her.

Miss Fitzpatrick probably wasn't the right person to ask. Sixty-something, her steel-gray hair wrenched into a prim bun, Miss Fitzpatrick was a caricature of the spinster schoolmarm, living with her elderly sisters and puttering to school in an ancient, pea-green Morris Minor that never went above thirty miles per hour. She always wore homemade, long-skirted Liberty-print dresses with a starched lace handkerchief attached to her lapel by a large safety pin. For thirteen- and fourteen-year-olds reveling in the rebellious atmosphere of the late 1960s, watching our elders scream, "Fuck the pigs!" at anti-Vietnam rallies, she should have been a gift from the gods: the ultimate fossil to satirize and send up.

Yet no one ever uttered a disrespectful word in her classroom. Other teachers had to bellow to get our attention. Miss Fitzpatrick could silence a class of rowdy adolescents with the raise of an eyebrow. When she read us the poetry of Verlaine and Ronsard, the room became so quiet that the only sound was the rhythmic pop of tennis balls from the courts outside. She transfixed us with French novels. When she read Antoine de St. Exupéry's memoir of his desert plane crash, I held my breath as she reached the passage where the downed pilot sees the nomad coming to his aid. In French, she read St. Exupéry's mellifluous paean to universal humanity and, looking up over the wire spectacles perched on her nose, translated it in her sweet, soft voice: "You are the well-loved brother. . . ." In the pause that followed, I wasn't the only one snuffling into my Kleenex.

Miss Fitzpatrick spoke French with an impeccable Parisian accent, and spun tales of regional life in Normandy and Provence as if she had supped on *soupe de poisson* in every portside café and cheered the boule players in every sycamore-shaded square. In fact, she had never left Australia.

Every afternoon, in French class, she drew us a little bit further into her illusory world. As the cicadas drummed in the eucalyptus trees outside the classroom window, I filled exercise books with essays on French culture so detailed that in one, on cuisine, I noted that a satisfactory accompaniment for *saumon au beurre blanc* would be a Puligny Montrachet 1961. The only salmon I had ever tasted had come out of a can, and wine, in our house, meant sweet sherry.

Unfortunately, when it came to the language itself, I didn't turn out to be the prodigy I'd hoped. I could read and write well enough, memorizing great swaths of obscure vocabulary. But when the words left the page and floated out into the air, they might as well have been Swahili. Because I learned words by writing them down, my brain stubbornly clung to the way their spelling was supposed to sound in English. And because I had trouble understanding correct pronunciations, I had trouble reproducing them. My spoken French was a raspy collection of diphthongs in which I habitually swallowed the consonants that should have been stressed and barked out the ones that were meant to remain silent.

When I told Miss Fitzpatrick that I wanted a French pen friend, she said she'd be delighted to help.

I forgot to mention Paris.

I had imagined fiery dispatches from the Paris barricades, scrawled in haste on table napkins. Instead, Janine wrote to me on delicate azure stationery, her letter folded as carefully as a piece of origami, her penmanship impeccable. Her address was a placid village in Vaucluse, Provence, a village so tiny I searched in vain for it on all the school library's maps of France. St. Martin de la Brasque, population 516, didn't even have a high school. Janine boarded during the week in a town called Manosque, near Marseilles, where the disciplinary regime sounded tougher, if possible, than the tyranny being exacted upon me in Concord.

In some ways her letters were a great advertisement for the French education system. Written half in French, half in English, they rarely contained a grammatical slip. Janine had started studying English two years earlier than we had begun French. After receiving my first letter, she kindly wrote that my French wasn't *très mauvais*. But then, she hadn't heard me try to speak it.

Her proletarian credentials, at least, seemed impeccable. Her father was a farmhand who made his living pruning and cultivating the vines of the Lubéron. The farmer's daughter in her showed an avid interest in Australian sheep populations and wheat-growing acreage. To my mortification, and in confirmation of my own worst fears, the only Australian culture she'd heard of was agriculture.

But when I probed her for working-class consciousness, all I got was a dissertation on the aggravating behavior of the *minets,* or *beaucoup snob,* who peopled her school. Instead of being feted for her peasant origins, as I imagined she would be among the Maoist student radicals of Paris, it seemed she was enduring a quiet torment from the bourgeois pupils at her boarding school.

It soon became clear that there wouldn't be any epistolary discussion of French philosophers. Janine wrote that she preferred "adventure books." But what really shocked me was the arrested state of her knowledge of popular culture. Janine had never heard of my heroes *du jour*, Leonard Cohen and Dustin Hoffman. Her knowledge of modern music ended with the Beatles. When I asked her about French cinema, she replied that she adored Brigitte Bardot. She had seen no Jean Renoir, no François Truffaut.

I stared at the charming valediction, "I kiss you on the two cheeks," and wondered at the paradox of one so French yet so unsophisticated.

In one letter Janine opined that the Côte d'Azur youths who experimented with drugs *sont idiots*. Since I was avidly tending the seedlings that had sprouted from my marijuana seeds, I found her views on this subject *pas sympathique*. Engaging as she was, Janine was no alter ego. Or at least not that year. I was longing to taste life and push limits, and I couldn't understand anyone my age who didn't feel the same.

But corresponding with Janine had done wonders for my cultural cringe. Sydney, it seemed, was nowhere near as cut off from the world as St. Martin de la Brasque. I began to consider that I might not be so close to the ends of the earth as I had always imagined.

My grandmother
Phyllis, the most
beautiful of
the O'Brien girls.

My great-grandmother,
the Boorowa midwife
Bridget O'Brien.

My mother, Gloria,
a radio announcer in Canberra.

My mother by a billabong in Boorowa with
two of her cousins during the Depression.

Portrait of Gloria Brooks.

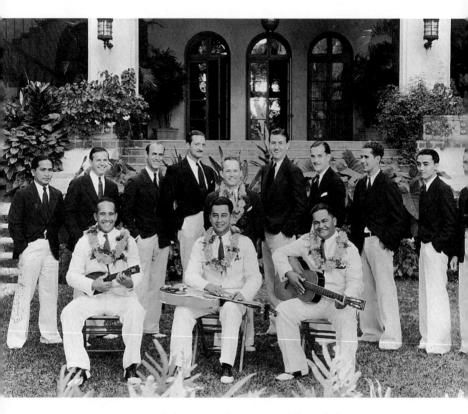

My father (standing, second from left) at
the Royal Hawaiian Hotel, circa 1935.

My father at the microphone
at radio station KGMB,
Honolulu, where
he hosted a show called
"Chasing the Blues" in
the early 1930s.

Concord, 1961.
Setting out for my first
day at school.

An evening on the front
verandah of
the Bland Street, Ashfield,
terrace house, 1957.

With my sister, Darleen,
at her sixth-grade Christmas
concert, 1959.

Nell "Sonny" Campbell (wearing hat) with sister Cressida, 1966.

Mishal at age sixteen, 1971.

Joannie in 1973 just before leaving for Vassar. On the back she writes, "This is a bad picture . . . makes me look fat."

Morneen Kamiki, Lawrie Brooks's
most important "pen pal."

7

Which Side
Are You On?

⌐⌐⌐

"Today's the day Nixon (aargh!) became President," wrote Joannie in her first letter of 1969. "We had to watch it in school just before lunch and it was absolutely repulsive. When Spiro T. Agnew came on screen everybody booed—nobody likes him. Then when Nixon was taking this oath, most everybody clapped but I hissed. My friend and I made this deal that we're never never NEVER going to call Nixon President. Just plain Nixon, but not P——— Nixon."

If Janine lacked adolescent rage, Joannie had plenty. She was burning mad about the war, about pollution ("Yesterday, air pollution levels were unhealthy for the 64th time this year. Fun"), and about the conservative tilt in American politics.

Joannie was exactly what I'd hoped for in a pen pal: her American life was right in the path of history. Both her brothers had been subject to the draft. One, the molecular biologist, was protected by his academic status, but the other had gone through the tortuous process of declaring himself a conscientious objector. Her sister lived in Berkeley and was friends with the members of Country Joe and the Fish, whose antiwar songs were famous even in Australia.

That year, to my ineffable envy, Joannie took her vacations in San Francisco and London, from whence she dispatched descriptions of the hippies. In Haight-Ashbury, she wrote, "there are lots of bearded guys strolling around in strange outfits. Some of the girls have on minis and some have long embroidered gowns. . . . They've got good views on peace." In Piccadilly Circus—"is it wild there! . . . all nationalities and varying degrees of cleanliness . . . great floppy felt hats are THE fashion there now—not so in America, where it's sunglasses. What's up in Australia?"

What was up, for me, was a pair of black faux-satin flared pants that I'd asked the Greek seamstress who lived across the road to make up for me. The pants were so wide around the ankles that the excess fabric flapped in the breeze like a deflated spinnaker. The top half of the outfit consisted of a serape my mother had helped me make out of a square of upholstery brocade with a piece of fringe sewn all around. When I put my head through the hole in the center, I looked like I'd been throttled by a sofa.

Darleen might have saved me from this fashion disaster, but from the distance of Melbourne, she was spared the sight of me. Mrs. Papas, the seamstress, tried her best. A statuesque woman with a high, heavy brow, her dark eyes surveyed me as I tried on the pants and attempted to walk without tripping over the wildly flapping hems. "Why you not let me make you very nice dress?" she said. "Better for you, more pretty."

But in 1969 I didn't want to be pretty. I wanted to be mysterious, wild, disheveled, disreputable. One snapshot taken that year perfectly captured my looking-for-trouble mood. I was gazing down, away from the camera, hair falling enigmatically across my face as I tried to achieve the pout of an alienated radical. I liked this picture so much I had copies made and sent them to all my pen pals. Their replies—a diplomatic *"Je te trouve très belle"* from Janine, a polite "You have a nice hair" from Mishal and a phlegmatic "Don't worry; you should see some of the pictures that get taken of me" from Joannie—indicated that I would have to work a little harder to achieve the desired impression.

Our inspiring school principal Sister Ruth had gone off on a mission to New York City where she'd spent time working in a literacy program in Harlem. When she returned, she addressed a school assembly. We stood there in the concrete playground, a sea of prim mauve school uniforms, as the summer sun beat down and caused patches of dark sweat to bloom on our backs and under our arms. Sister Ruth talked passionately of the hardships of lives in the ghetto and the courage of the civil rights movement. She wanted us to take from her speech a sense of how lucky we were in our tranquil, privileged country. Instead, I longed to be a Freedom Rider in Montgomery or a Yippie in Chicago.

I turned fifteen as the sixties came to a close. The country was at war and thousands of young people were routinely getting their heads busted in the streets of the cities for protesting Australia's involvement. I spent my days at school on Bland Street, convinced that history was happening without me.

In fact, little pieces of history were moving in all around me. The Serbs next door were survivors of the fascist Ustasha. The elderly White Russian spinster at the top of our street had fled the revolution with her family and spent her girlhood in Manchuria. The Turk over the back fence had lived through two coups. Mrs. Papas's Greek family had felt the heavy hand of the military junta.

At the end of the sixties, it remained more fashionable to laugh at immigrants than to listen to them. When the Papas family moved into a tiny liver-brick cottage across the road, they covered it with white stucco and replaced its veranda with a columned portico—turning it into a sad little parody of the ancient island homes they'd left behind.

It was intellectually chic, in the 1960s, to make fun of the Greeks' penchant for stucco and the Italians' propensity for covering every surface in aquamarine or flamingo pink. It was part of a mocking riff against Australian lower-middle-class suburban life, which was invariably portrayed as empty, vapid, philistine.

The few publications that addressed Australian reality were utterly contemptuous of the section of it that I inhabited. "Behold the man—the Australian man of today—on Sunday mornings in the suburbs. . . . A block of land, a brick veneer, and the motor-mower beside him in the wilderness—what more does he want to sustain him . . . ?" wrote Allan Ashbolt in the mainstream intellectual journal *Meanjin.* The flagship of the alternative press, *Oz* magazine, was even more cutting—dismissing all inhabitants of the sprawl as undifferentiated idiots named Alf whose lives passed without drama or passion or deep emotion of any kind. Towering literary figures such as Patrick White joined in the chorus of disdain. In *The Road from Coorain,* Jill Ker Conway writes in loving detail of the places she lived. But when her family is forced by strapped finances to move for a time to my slice of Sydney—an "unfashionable, lower-middle-class suburb to the west of the city"—she dispatches the experience within a page and a half and does not even give the suburb's name.

Barry Humphries, a cruel and brilliant satirist, appeared on stage as "Edna Everage," a suburban housewife who loves gladiolus, decorates her walls with plaster flying ducks and aspires to cruise-ship vacations. After attending one of his revues, I was mortified that we too had plaster ducks formation-flying across our sitting-room wall. The next time my mother asked me to dust, I "accidentally" dropped one, wrecking the set and causing my mother to take them down.

A few minutes' independent reflection on what I knew about where I lived would have exposed the superficiality of these caricatures. Even our humble neighbor Edna, whose very name was a joke to Humphries, was a survivor of betrayal whose day-to-day good humor was evidence of the existence of grace. When her husband walked out on her, leaving her penniless with two sons to raise, the Catholic Church asked her to make a choice. If she ever remarried, the priest told her, she would never be able to take Communion. By choosing the Church, she condemned herself to a lonely, frugal life, taking in spinster borders to make ends meet. But over all the "cuppas" she shared with my mother, I never once heard her complain.

As for Mrs. Papas, the seamstress, her life was a modern Greek tragedy. Exiled in her girlhood to a land at the end of the earth so her wages could send a brother to school; married without her consent to a man her intellectual inferior; terrified of the blood on her wedding night, with no one who spoke her language there to reassure her; waking one morning to realize her husband hadn't come home and finding herself unable to persuade cynical policemen that he was really missing, not adulterously AWOL; finally hearing, months later, that his body had been found in an abandoned railyard.

The intellectuals of *Oz* and *Meanjin* could be forgiven for poking fun at such people for seeming to settle for the small life of the suburbs. They didn't know my neighbors' stories.

It is less easy to forgive myself.

"I've been passing around petitions against Nixon's invasion of Cambodia," Joannie wrote in May 1970. "I was sent to the office for passing one around in school (would you believe you need permission . . . ?)"

Yes, I believed it. At my school it suddenly seemed as though you needed permission to sneeze. Not long after the assembly at which she'd told us about her work in the New York ghettos, Sister Ruth disappeared. No announcement was made, but whispers soon passed word that she had left the convent. It made sense to me: how could Bland Street hold on to someone who had walked the mean streets of Harlem? My feverish imagination conjured a romance with a handsome Black Panther, and I visualized Ruth, nun's habit banished, wafting through the ghetto in flowing Indian prints.

Other favorite nuns also disappeared. Sister Gabriella, who had used religion classes to open our eyes to apartheid and to our own disgraceful history with Australian Aborigines, went to work in a pub and was married in no time.

The nuns who remained hunkered down in defensive reaction. The new principal was no firebrand feminist. Before you could say "Bless me, Father" we were back in the Dark Ages. Assemblies designed to open our minds to human rights and social activism were swiftly replaced with harangues on the proper way to wear our uniforms so as not to call attention to our bustlines.

But our minds had been touched beyond the reach of this attempted counterrevolution. The lay staff from Sister Ruth's era remained, teaching us to ask the very questions that the new regime wished to avoid. An exchange teacher arrived from the United States and seemed stunned by how reserved and inarticulate we all were. She urged us to discuss things, to jump in with comments without raising our hands. She had grown up on a farm in Ohio, and she described her life there in fascinating detail.

At fifteen, I had never seen a farm. For all the mystique of the Outback, Australians are among the most urbanized people in the world, with more than ninety percent of the population crowded into the six large coastal cities. Never having been west of the Blue Mountains, the Outback was a rumor to me. My images were gleaned from my mother's descriptions of Boorowa, embellished with vague clichés about remote sheep stations the size of Belgium where children got their schooling by short-wave radio and doctors arrived by plane.

Ohio's patchwork of small family holdings sounded cozy— like something in a storybook. But the teacher talked also of the stifling conservatism of Midwestern rural life and how difficult it was to be a nonconformist in a community where the local church was the center of your social world. Once again, I came face to face with the fact that Sydney, for all its distance, was more culturally diverse than many other places in which I might have been set down.

Not long before she vanished, Sister Ruth hired the school's first male teacher. Anybody else might have introduced men to our cloistered world gently, with a tweedy geriatric or two. But Sister Ruth chose Mr. Bishop, a twenty-something drop-dead-gorgeous blond with long hair and a Zapata mustache. Of course I fell in love with him. We all did. Somehow, he managed to keep an unswelled head and a straight face, as adolescents hitched up their mauve uniforms and swooned in his path.

Sister Ruth had chosen him because he happened to be an inspired teacher. Until his arrival, the geography syllabus's dull fixation on population statistics and lists of principal crops had bored me stiff. But Mr. Bishop had been to the places he talked about. When he taught us about New Guinea, it wasn't in *National Geographic* images of men in bird-of-paradise headdresses. He told of slogging through viscous mud to meet tribes whose hunting grounds had been laid waste by international mining companies. He described the status of women in many highland villages—somewhere below the status of pigs. Mr. Bishop connected the wiring between my fascination with Elsewhere and the facts to be had in the geography textbooks.

He also taught English, introducing us to off-the-syllabus

poets such as Wilfred Owen, whose antiwar poems opened my eyes to the fact that our generation hadn't invented pacifism.

I wrote to Joannie about Mr. Bishop, and she was gratifyingly impressed. "<u>My</u> English teacher this year is bowlegged, funnyfaced, and a staunch conservative anti-communist. He tries to indoctrinate us in class—'You just can't let Communists stay around—if you let one germ live it'll multiply and soon the whole world will be taken over.' Etcetera. I have had a strong temptation to say 'Bullshit' to his face several times, but I generally don't curse and besides if I told him that, I can imagine what grade I would receive."

I understood her predicament. Despite my radical pretensions, I was doing quite well at the hands of the evil Establishment. I'd won a government scholarship that was paying all my school expenses. My painting of a melting face, heavily influenced by the psychedelic poster art of San Francisco, had taken first prize at the Ashfield art exhibition. That winter my mother and father and I vacationed in Tasmania—the first time any of us had been on a plane. It was a trip I'd won in a Young Reporters' Contest run by the national newspaper, the *Australian*.

That year, also, our debating team won the final of the citywide tournament by arguing for the proposition "That Science Is a Menace." I could argue with some feeling, because another prize I'd hoped to win, in the statewide science fair, had certainly created a menace to my mother's mental health. My project, to prove the food value of certain common garden weeds, had required keeping mice. My mother's lifelong fear of the rodents lost the war with her desire to encourage all my academic endeavors. Even though the project only required adding small amounts of nontoxic weed to the mice's diet each week and weighing them to see if they continued to thrive, I couldn't face actually experimenting on an animal. So I volunteered to care for the control group.

Joannie, who had been keeping mice for four years, sent me reams of advice: "I feed my mice a mixture of birdseed, oatmeal, and cornmeal all swished together, plus a little lettuce for each mouse, and a dog biscuit once a week. . . . They like shredded paper towel to make a nest in, or a small cardboard box. Don't give them newspaper because the ink will rub off on their fur and they'll eat it while attempting to clean themselves."

In thanks, I named one of the control mice Joannie, although since all were albinos I had difficulty telling her apart from the others: Spock, Rudolph and Margot (the latter two named for a balletomane phase I was passing through).

"Do you know that I never had a mouse named for me before? I was very flattered—and to have my name in such a company of distinguished persons!" Joannie, of course, had already had several Spocks in her mice cages: "Mr. Spock the first (black and white) who lived to be almost two years old and died last 8 August 1969, when we were in Europe. Mr. Spock the second was eaten by his mother before his eyes even opened. Now I have Mr. Spock the third (black) who'll be a year old on October 12. Long live the Spocks!"

Unfortunately, my Mr. Spock met a grisly end, along with the noble attempt to alleviate world hunger and the run at the science prize. The project fell apart when my mice—the control group, fed on the gourmet mouse mix—began eating each other. The day we gave away the sole—and very fat—survivor of my doomed experiment was a happy one for my mother. Joannie was consoling: "Perhaps you just had paranoid mice."

Joannie probably could have gotten away with saying "Bullshit" to her English teacher. Her high school seemed to be in the kind of tumult where a few "bullshits" here or there wouldn't have been noticed. Her first letter of 1971 contained an account of a performance in the school assembly hall of a band called Voice of America—"They used amplifiers and light boxes and electric guitars. . . . I had to get up and leave because the sound was really murdering my ears. . . . Just before I left, there was a disturbance on stage; a couple of students wanted to make an announcement about how they had been unjustly treated. A couple of teachers dragged them off. Now the whole school is in uproar about it."

She sent me copies of the student samizdat being passed around. One poorly typed handout was addressed:

TO ALL THOSE SMOKING IN THE BATHROOMS (and we ain't just talking about cigarettes either).
. . . has it ever occured to you why the school talks about getting draft counseling but never does get it? they know that if enough people took a look at the draft, they would find it immoralx if you are 18 youx z can vote for the president of the u.s., and fight in a war and kill or be killed, yet you cant walk the halls or go to the bathroom with out a pass. . . . what it xallx comes down to is you are either part of the problem or part of the solution, which side are you on? do you want to lead the zombie life: black suit and tie, nine to five, five days a week, sipping martinis on the 8o"clock train to the big city . . .

Those who wished to be part of the solution were urged to attend a meeting about it. "Only 35 people showed up," wrote Joannie in disgust. It seemed that most of the Maplewood students didn't mind the idea of sipping martinis after all.

But Joannie was despairing about the state of her country. "When I grow up, if I ever get a chance to, I'm getting out of America as fast as I possibly can and moving to Austria or England or somesuch." She began adding little editorial comments to the return address in the top left-hand corner of her envelopes: "United States of Amerika," or "U.S.A. (unfortunately)."

Every summer, when school let out, the postmark on her letters signaled her presence in yet another exotic location. "The clouds are just lifting from the mountain tops" she wrote in the summer of 1971, from a town named Visp in Switzerland where she was summering with a family as part of a student exchange program. In July 1972 her address was Salzburg, where she was taking intensive German classes at the American Institute for Foreign Study. Then she was on a train back to Switzerland with Dolfi, the boy from the family she'd stayed with the previous year: "He's what I guess would be called my summer boyfriend, and would be my winter boyfriend too, if only possible!"

Again, I was desperately envious. At sixteen, I was just beginning to be allowed to see boys, but only at home or on group outings to carefully screened activities. Chaperones and curfews hedged every move. The idea of being free to travel across Europe with a boyfriend seemed wildly, impossibly romantic.

By August, Joannie was back in the States, writing from a town named Menemsha. Her postcards showed dazzling sunsets on a reach of tranquil water. It looked like a scenic spot, but the rest of the address—"Martha's Vineyard, Mass."—meant nothing to me. "We have a house and a cabin here, right next to each other . . . the cabin is just a cabin, one room, with two beds in it, which I took over two years ago and have since redecorated. . . . I'm working on some new curtains for it now. . . . Then it's back to school on September 6 . . . the fact that it's an election year should lend some interest. I'm still for McGovern even though he did make a mess of the Eagleton affair, but I don't think he'll win. . . ."

Nineteen seventy-two was also an election year in Australia. For once the result was in doubt, largely because of Australian involvement in the Vietnam War. A bureaucrat's careless prediction that the venture would buy U.S. goodwill without "dispro-portionate expenditure" now had its exact price: four hundred and ninety-four Australians had died, many of them conscripts too young to vote against the government sending them to war.

For the first time in decades, the Labor Party had a charis-matic leader, Gough Whitlam, to articulate popular rage and frustration. Whitlam was a witty barrister with a classicist's breadth of knowledge. Almost six and a half feet tall, he tow-ered both literally and figuratively over the Liberal pygmies who had succeeded Menzies (who had finally retired at the age of seventy-one).

On election night, December 2, we sat glued to the TV as the ballot-count came in. For once, my father had backed a winner. Like millions of Australians, we celebrated.

It is no exaggeration to say Australia changed overnight. Whitlam immediately ended conscription, freed jailed draft dodgers and ordered the troops home from Vietnam. Wages and welfare payments rose. Aborigines got real say in their own affairs. Women got equal pay. The voting age was lowered to eighteen from twenty-one. The arts began to receive an unprece-dented infusion of government funding. Whitlam introduced universal health insurance, doubled education spending, abol-ished university fees and established generous allowances for students who needed them. "God Save the Queen" ceased to be our national anthem, and we stopped shunning countries like Cuba and China just because the Americans told us to.

Every day, under Whitlam, Australia seemed to become more itself and less a pale imitation of elsewhere. Gardening shows began to address how to plant banksias rather than box-woods. Art exhibitions featured Australian painters rather than imports. Australian movies started to reflect our own reality and our own sense of fantasy. Genuine Australian accents replaced elocution-lesson English on the radio and television.

It is a great thing, at seventeen, to learn that it's possible to change the world. I started my last year of high school knowing that if I did well I would go to university without financial hardship. When I wrote my return address on letters to my pen pals, I was proud that I lived in such a progressive place. For the first time in my life, there was nowhere else I'd rather be.

8

Same Place,
Different Skies

~~~∞◦∞~~~

"Dear Geraldine,

"Hi!

"Would you believe I'm so uninformed I hadn't heard of the
government changeover in Australia?" wrote Joannie on January 10, her first letter of 1973. I was used to the historic happen-
ings of my homeland never making a ripple past our own
shores. But Joannie had a different excuse for missing the news.

"I'm sort of shut off from the outside world where I am
now—at the hospital. I think I may have mentioned to you a
few months ago that I was on a diet—well, I sort of carried it
too far."

I hadn't bothered to look at the envelope. But there in the
top corner was the return address: Memorial Unit, Yale-New
Haven Hospital. Joannie wrote that she had collapsed three days
before Christmas and arrived at the hospital emergency room
"unconscious, dehydrated, in shock, and with a blood pressure
of 40/?"

Almost three weeks later she was, she wrote, "a lot better,

am up and around and gaining weight, but still I will probably be here for 3 months or so."

It sounded like an odd sort of hospital. "There are a lot of other patients my age, including some very nice boys"—after which she'd drawn a smiley face—"and the doctors and nurses are all wonderful too. We are kept very busy by all sorts of meetings and activities . . . and I'm beginning to learn a lot about myself, and a lot about other people too."

I didn't know what to make of this. If Joannie had lost too much weight, surely all she had to do was eat more. Why would she have to spend three months in a hospital? How could she take the time, in the middle of her crucial senior year?

In January 1973, I had never heard the words "anorexia nervosa." The self-starvation that would become an epidemic of female adolescence was still little known in the United States and wasn't yet discussed at all in Australia.

Like many Australians, I had been raised to be suspicious of neurosis. Ours was the sentiment so perfectly articulated in the movie *Crocodile Dundee,* when Mick Dundee meets a woman at a New York party who has seen a psychiatrist. Mick, alarmed, assumes she's crazy. His American girlfriend tries to explain that the woman isn't mad, she just needed to see a psychiatrist to talk over her problems. "Hasn't she got any mates?" responds Mick. To an American audience, that's a gag line. To Australians it's a sensible query.

My mother, in particular, despised what she considered the navel-gazing of psychotherapy. To her, neurosis was nothing but self-pity indulged until it had run amok. She had mild claustrophobia that made her panic when pulling a sweater over her head. Going into elevators was a penance, yet she forced herself to ride them; she never took the stairs. "You have to fight your fears," she said.

I had my own neuroses, although I didn't think of them that way. Whenever our debating team traveled to a competitor school, my first stop was the bathroom, so I could throw up. When I started going out on dates, I threw up during those, too. I had inherited my father's stage fright, but it was stage fright amplified by the terrible adolescent delusion that I was walking around lit up by a spotlight, and that every gaffe I made was noticed by the whole world.

It would never have occurred to me to try to get help with this. "Stop dwelling on yourself," my mother said. "Think about how the other person is feeling instead." My mother also said what always is said to adolescents: "Everyone goes through it. Everyone feels like you do."

Of course, I didn't believe her. I certainly didn't believe that Joannie—my well-traveled pen pal who had recently been elected class president—could be battling the same tide of insecurity that was tugging at me.

I don't know exactly what I wrote back to Joannie, but I suspect it was something Pollyanaish, with a "look on the bright side" tone. Her reply, on January 23, began brightly in response. "I just finished playing Ping Pong with my favorite one of those 'nice boys' you mentioned in your last letter ☺!"

But after a few polite queries about my vacation plans, the facade of cheerfulness soon fell away. "I was accepted last year at Vassar College, and had been planning to go in September '73. But now I'm not really sure, mainly because of the hospitalization." In 1973, I had heard of a handful of Ivy League schools—names like Harvard, Yale or Princeton would have meant something to me. I hadn't heard of Vassar, so the extent of Joannie's achievement in getting admitted to such a fine college was lost on me. And that meant I also missed an important signal as to the seriousness of her illness: that she was considering passing up such a prize.

"I don't know if college right away would be the best thing

for me," she wrote. "There's a lot of talking with everybody to be done." Some of the talking took place Saturdays and Wednesdays, when Joannie's parents made the five-hour round-trip drive from Maplewood to take part in "Family Meetings." Patients, their relatives and the staff talked about "family difficulties, or problems they have in common, or what have you."

Over the years, Joannie had written a lot about her brothers and sister, and had warmly mentioned her mother a number of times. But she had never said anything about her father. She had never even told me what he did for a living. It was an odd lacuna in a correspondence as detailed as ours. All I knew was that his work had taken them to live in both Washington, D.C., and Austria for a time.

Now, given the hints she was dropping of family strife, my overactive imagination began conjuring scenarios for its causes. I knew that Austria, in those Cold War days, was a key espionage base for spies operating behind the Iron Curtain. Perhaps Joannie's father was a CIA agent. It would explain her silence on the matter; also, given her left-wing politics, it would account for bitter feeling between them. My theory thrilled me: I rolled it around in my head, thinking up clever questions that would allow me to test it.

Joannie's next letter mentioned her father, but only in the context of a package I'd sent containing books, bangles, rings and incense. "The incense even my father liked, and usually he hates the smell of it." (Perhaps because it reminded him of nefarious CIA doings in Southeast Asia?)

It was early March, and Joannie was writing from home: "I am finally out of the hospital and am going to school again. I have been so glad to see all of my friends!" They had thrown a welcome-home party for her. She was glad to be back in school. The class vice-president had been particularly pleased to see her—"he decided he wasn't cut out for the job of President. As for me, I can hardly wait, I love the job, although it's a lot of work, but the sense of responsibility is really good for me." Aside from worrying about how she was going to make up all her missed schoolwork, Joannie sounded like her old, ebullient self again. Her letter ended with the news that her Swiss boyfriend Dolfi "is coming over this summer in July—cheers!"

Whatever dark clouds had settled on Joannie that past December, they seemed to have lifted. By May, she wrote that she had firmly decided to start college in the fall. "They have sent me all sorts of forms to fill out, and naturally I'm very nervous, but I suppose that everyone is. Where do you plan on going?"

I planned on going to the University of Sydney, Australia's oldest institution of higher learning. The heart of the campus was a beautiful collection of colonnaded Gothic buildings modeled on Oxford colleges. For years, riding the bus to and from the city, I'd passed the big stone gates and dreamed of entering them.

The only question was whether my marks in the public exam at the end of the year would be high enough. In Australia, marks were all that mattered. There were no selection committees, no personal interviews, no account taken of where one's parents had gone or how much money they'd given the alumni fund. A computer matched your marks with your preferences, and the numbers made the decision. I'd done the work, and I loved exams the way a crossword addict loves a puzzle. Unless a bus hit me en route to the exam hall, I had every reason to believe that when the Australian academic year started the following February, I'd get my wish.

Joannie and I went back to comparing notes on politics, good books and music. All mention of eating disorders and group therapy disappeared from her letters. She had big plans for college, including a junior year abroad in a German-speaking country and a scheme, the summer following, to "fly from Europe to Australia. How does that sound?"

It sounded great to me. My own plans to travel abroad were

still years in the future, so I jumped at the idea of finally meeting Joannie on my own turf. I imagined showing her my beautiful city, and maybe taking a trip to discover the Outback together.

Meanwhile, we continued to compare notes on our current lives. Mine, as the make-or-break exam approached, was consumed by academic effort. I lived between King Lear's blasted heath and Bernini's soaring baldachino; my mind rang with Goering edicts and Gide poetics.

Joannie, with her college admission in the bag, was having a far more relaxing year. We compared reading lists for our English classes. "I haven't read Return of the Native, The Dubliners, Emma or Tree of Man," Joannie wrote. "Maybe I'm illiterate. What I am rereading for school now is The Lord of the Rings, which is as good as ever." I loved *Lord of the Rings*. At thirteen, I'd carried my copy to school and read it under the desk until caught during a geography lesson. But I was surprised that this entertaining fantasy was considered serious fare for senior-year literary study.

In the United States, Watergate was breaking. "I watched the Nixon speech with friends and we all nearly died laughing," she wrote of the "I am not a crook" debacle. "I don't think he'll get impeached but he'll never live this down, either. I hope he loses a lot of his power over Congress. Seemingly that is beginning to happen because both the House and the Senate recently passed a bill to stop all bombing in Indochina."

In Australia, Whitlam's new government was doing all it could to stop the bombing too. A few years earlier, Australia had pledged to go "all the way with LBJ." Now our leaders branded the Christmas blitz of Hanoi as the act of "maniacs" and "mass murderers." I was so proud of Whitlam's stand. For the first time, I felt that a politician actually spoke for me. I felt sorry for Joannie, still stuck with a leader of whom she was ashamed.

. . .

In August, Joannie was once again writing from Martha's Vineyard. It was there, a year earlier, that her problems had begun. Perhaps being back triggered something again. Her first letter from the island contained disturbing hints that everything wasn't quite right. Inside the envelope was a snapshot of Joannie with her two-year-old niece. "This is a bad picture . . . makes me look fat" she wrote on the back of the photograph. I turned over the picture. It actually made her look thin—slender, leggy, beautiful, with the swanlike neck I'd always envied.

"I guess I didn't tell you or maybe you forgot, but I am changing my name." She had decided, she wrote, to take her mother's maiden name. Since she was as much entitled to her mother's surname as her father's, she wrote, "why can't I have the name I want?"

She would be leaving for college on the fifteenth of September. "I'll send you my address as soon as I know it. I'll be living in a dormitory where they'll hopefully allow me to bring my mice." She was enrolling as a premed student. "The course I am most nervous about is General Biology because I am afraid I will not be able to keep up with the rest of the class. I am also nervous about what I will do in my spare time as I often have difficulty in getting myself to go out and do things."

Her Swiss boyfriend Dolfi had been with her all summer. "It sounds like a fantastic set-up but it hasn't worked out so well, mainly because my feelings have changed. He's really an awfully sweet and understanding person, and that makes me feel horribly guilty. . . . He's incredibly active and always doing things and trying to keep up with him puts an awful lot of strain on me. Sometimes I do try, when I'm feeling good, but sometimes I honestly can't stand the sight of him and then I go off by myself. He's flying back on 22 August and I feel split. . . . Well, write soon, and have fun with your guy, at least. What's his name?"

• • •

His name was Duff: a long-haired university student whose smiling eyes had etched wonderful crow's-feet into his tan. I'd won his heart by leading a party that scaled the towering, barbed-wire-topped walls of the Sydney Showground to break into a sold-out Led Zeppelin concert. The fact that I was wearing a floor-length tie-dyed evening dress at the time must have added to my allure.

There was tremendous cachet in having a uni student for a boyfriend when one was still at school. I loved to meet him at the university to catch a film-society screening and sit sipping coffee on the balcony of the Union theater. Duff was a government major, so we had long political discussions in between rolling around on the soft grass of the university quad, kissing till our mouths ached.

He was also a pothead of serious proportions. My own venture into "grow-your-own" had come to an untimely end just months after it began. My father came wandering into the kitchen one Saturday morning after mowing the lawn. He had a puzzled expression on his face and a leaf of one of my precious plants in his hand. At work the day before, he'd proofread an article on how to identify cannabis. "Do you think we should call the police?" he said.

My mother grasped the situation instantly. She shot me one of her patented glares that could peel paint off brickwork. Then, rearranging her face into an expression of benign indifference, she turned to my father, took the leaf from his hand and deposited it in the kitchen tidy. "Don't be a mug, Daddy. It's just a weed. Reminds me, I was planning to clean up the side garden. Never seem to have time to get to it. Maybe this afternoon. Aren't the begonias blooming beautifully right now?"

Duff's supply line of what he called "dakka" didn't run

through the parental backyard and was seemingly inexhaustible. After several years of enforced abstinence, I leaped at this second chance to become a substance abuser. But my lungs still wouldn't tolerate the smoke. I coughed like a consumptive and never absorbed enough to get high. So I sat through the parties, cross-legged and closed-eyed, pretending to groove on the over-amplified base line of Iron Butterfly and the Aztecs—an Aussie band Duff loved to play at painful decibels. Before long, his turn for the Big Trip Elsewhere took him off on travels to Southeast Asia. I moped over his departure, but it probably saved my hearing.

Joannie's next letter came from Poughkeepsie, New York, from a dorm named Davison at Vassar College. I was months away from learning if I'd been accepted to the university, and almost half a year from actually starting classes. So I was curious to hear how Joannie was enjoying the experience.

It was 11 P.M., she wrote, and she was sitting with a bunch of fellow freshmen she'd just befriended. "My room is a single, which I don't really like, which is why I'm writing this letter with 3 other people in room 208 instead of shutting myself off in 211." It sounded cozy and collegiate. "Mike is reading Tolkien, Anita is reading Biology, Bill is reading economics and I have just finished reading 2 chapters of Saul Bellow's *Seize the Day* for English." It was the evening of her first full day of classes. "I can see I'm going to have to work awfully hard here, especially if I continue as a pre-med student. I really wonder if I can do it. . . . Write soon and enjoy yourself—Peace, Joannie."

I didn't have much time to enjoy myself at that point, with the matriculation exams looming and my last days as a high school student drawing to a close. I don't think I even had time to reply to her letter. With the exams finally over, I bought Joannie a silver chain for Christmas and sent it off with an apology for my tardy correspondence.

And so it was December before I learned that Joannie had almost died. Just two weeks after she'd written to me from her Vassar dorm, Joannie went home for the weekend and took an overdose of an antidepressant drug, Tofranil. She was rushed to intensive care as the doctors battled to save her life. After several days in the coronary care unit, she was admitted to a psychiatric clinic in Belle Mead, New Jersey, in a deep depression.

By early November she'd climbed out enough to be allowed home, but when she wrote to me late that month, the tone of her letter was strangely flat, as if she was still in the grip of a lingering sadness. "I will probably be going back to school next semester, although not to Vassar," she wrote. "I would be attending a local college and living at home." In the meantime, she had a volunteer job at a local hospital—"it gives me something to do." She thanked me for the silver chain: "I never used to wear jewelry. . . . I went through my Mr. Spock phase and decided jewelry was illogical and superfluous."

It seemed like such a long time since we'd both played at being the emotionless Vulcan. Now, Joannie was in the grip of emotions so overpowering they risked destroying her.

I worried when Joannie skipped her usual New Year's letter. Remembering that the previous holiday season had been the beginning of her hospitalization, I wrote inquiring how she was, and I worried as weeks passed without a reply.

It was almost the end of February before a letter arrived. It was a long letter, written over several sheets in a tiny, crabbed handwriting that I didn't even recognize. She'd started writing it late at night on the second of February.

"Hi. Sorry about not writing for so long—I've been going through sheer hell mentally and don't know if I feel like writing about it in detail—I have taken to wearing a silver crucifix which my great grandmother gave my mother. I wear it to remind me there is love in the world amidst all the self-hatred I feel for myself. Anyway, I use the silver chain you gave me for it—thanks again."

She was, she said, battling to retain some semblance of a normal life, having started at a local college in late January on a three-day-a-week schedule. "Because of my mental difficulties, I am having problems in concentrating and going, but basically the classes are interesting."

She had also managed to pass her driving test—"a sign of independence and adulthood, which is important for me, since that's part of my whole problem." The letter broke off at the end of the page. It began again four days later. It had been snowing. Joannie had always loved the cold and the snow—it had been an ongoing joke in our letters, because to me any temperature below sixty degrees was a torment, while she complained bitterly if winter didn't bring blizzards. Now, she said, she hated and feared the snow and the cold "because I feel it so intensely because I am so skinny and also I guess it has bad psychological representations to me to." That tiny misspelling— "to" for "too"—jumped off the page. Joannie was a meticulous writer who rarely made a grammar or spelling mistake.

At that point in the letter her handwriting changed abruptly. "I am going to start printing—it may be easier for you to read. I am having a hard time (physically) writing because I am so tense."

And I was having a hard time reading this outpouring of painful emotion. Until now, Joannie had written to me after she had climbed out of her depressions. As a result, I hadn't felt the full force of her despair. I'd let myself believe that Joannie was going through a bad phase that would eventually pass. It had seemed impossible to me that her intelligence wouldn't some-how lead her out of the emotional thicket in which she was temporarily lost.

For a few paragraphs, her letter covered familiar turf, with a critique of the state of the Union—confidence in the President at an all-time low of twenty-six per cent, the energy crisis, inflation, a truckers' strike, problems in the Middle East. But instead of her usual wry assessment, this time the catalogue of problems seemed to weigh upon her personally and add to her affliction.

"Part of me has just stopped fighting and I've got to find it and get it going again—it frightens me that I can't find it. Geraldine, I like you—that's reason enough to want to live, isn't it? I've got to find my will to live and give it a kick—I need some motivation. There are a lot of things I could hold onto but nothing seems to matter right now."

It was another nine days before Joannie was able to finish the letter. "I have already taken two Valium (a calming pill) tonight and as a result am feeling kind of wiped out. The depression in me makes me not want to go to school, the fright in me is sure I can't do the work, my various hang ups prevent me from doing the work, and everything is all messed up." She had called her psychiatrist and would be going by his office at 8 A.M. the next morning "so he can give me a shot of some sort to make me hopefully feel better."

I hoped her psychiatrist knew what he was doing. Surely this seesaw of downers and uppers risked making everything much worse. "I hope by the next letter to be able to paint a cheerier picture but I just can't write any more now. Take care of yourself, write soon, and I will try to write you back as soon as I can."

I read and reread the letter, trying to frame a reply. She had said that my friendship was a reason to live. I wanted to yell, "Yes! Yes! You're my oldest friend! We're going to do great things together one day. Don't you dare think of checking out!" I wanted to write something that would reach her and pull her out of her dark place. I wanted my letter to be as reassuring as an enfolding hug.

And yet there was another small voice in the back of my head—a querulous, no-nonsense voice saying: "Snap out of it. Fight your fears. Everyone goes through it. Stop thinking about yourself all the time." It was my mother's voice. Without even noticing, I had absorbed her belief that neurosis was the self-inflicted wound of the coward who can't face the fight. Deep down, there was a small, ungenerous part of me that didn't empathize with Joannie, a tiny kernel of contempt for her weakness.

Earlier that month I had finally walked through the big stone gates of Sydney University. I'd arrived there brimming with confidence, proud of good exam results.

But the exhilaration didn't last long. Drifting from one big anonymous lecture hall to the other, I soon felt lost and lonely at the university. My Bland Street school had been a safe, intimate environment full of people just like me—same gender, same socioeconomic level, same religious background. The vast arts faculty of the University of Sydney was a different story. I had thought I would love the diversity, but instead I felt over-whelmed by it. I was in awe of the students from the private schools of the North Shore and the eastern suburbs who seemed to have so much poise and polish. I wasn't sure how to act in front of the young men in my classes. The English department was huge; the fine arts department snobbish.

The only place I felt comfortable was the government de-partment. I'd taken the subject as an afterthought because Duff had said it had good lecturers. Many of them were Americans—disenchanted veterans of the 1960s culture wars. One, who de-scribed himself as a "Lyndon Johnson Canadian," had left his country to dodge the draft.

But my shyness made it an ordeal to speak up in tutorials. I might have gone through the year in silence if it hadn't been for the only-in-Australia custom of some of the younger tutors, who liked to hold their tutorials in the beer gardens of the various pubs near the uni. I soon found that a swiftly downed boiler-maker made it possible for me to barge into any discussion without inhibition. Because of Australians' cultural acceptance of drinking—even of drinking to excess—it never occurred to me to question what I was doing.

But even with the alcohol buffer, the university became bleaker as the seasons changed. In late summer, when the lawns were still covered with clusters of students laughing together or arguing over their books, I had been able to imagine myself eventually becoming part of such a group. But as the cooler weather drove the students inside and rain stripped the foliage from the sycamores, I wandered alone from class to class over the slick, blackened leaves and despaired of ever finding a friend.

"Snap out of it! You don't know how lucky you are." My mother, the voice of reason, had little patience with my morose-ness. "When I was a kid I was so shy I didn't just have trouble speaking to strangers—I used to cross the street so I wouldn't have to say hello to people I knew." My mother had dealt with her shyness by getting a job in radio, where she spoke to thou-sands of strangers at a time. Her prescription was simple: find the thing you are most afraid of, then go and do it.

I was afraid to be noticed, to speak up in public. The last time I'd visited Darleen in Melbourne, she'd had a photographer friend from the advertising agency take some nice pictures of me. So, looking for an antidote like my mother's, I made an appointment with a Sydney casting agent, to see if I had any chance of getting work as an extra in commercials or TV shows. Within a few weeks I had more jobs than I could handle.

Instead of moping around the campus in between classes, I sped off to shoots all over the city. I played a biker's moll (in a bad movie called *Sidecar Boys*), an eighteenth-century French aristocrat (in an ad for ice cream), a mountain climber (Deep Heat liniment), a dancing groupie (Bacardi and Coke) and—my favorite role—a steer-roping, canoe-racing nun (in a TV comedy called "Flash Nick from Jindavik").

These jobs gave me the nerve to audition for a tiny part in a production by SUDS, the Sydney University Dramatic Society. At the first rehearsal I glimpsed a tall blond in white overalls wandering around discussing lighting and props. He was the stage manager. Someone introduced us, and when he smiled at me it was like the sun coming out. Trevor was an architect, designing buildings for the government by day, studying for his degree at night.

Being in love made everything easy. The Gothic buildings of the university once again looked beautiful instead of daunting, and by September, as the weather warmed, I was sprawled on the sunny lawn, laughing with my friends from the drama society.

With everything going so well, it became hard to write to Joannie. I didn't want to dwell on how good my life was, when hers was still so precarious. And yet if I didn't tell her what I was doing it left very little to say.

Her replies were warmly enthusiastic. "Twenty years from now I will be able to boast that I possess a piece of correspondence from the world-renowned actress Geraldine Brooks!" she joked when I wrote to her about my jobs as an extra. During her college vacation she was working at the local swimming pool snack bar. "The work keeps me busy, which is important, and it's generally fun."

But the battle with her weight continued. "I was down to 69 lbs. but that was about a month and a half ago . . . now I'm up to 74 and feel much better."

I had to get out a calculator and work out her weight in

kilograms before I could make sense of this. I weighed forty-five kilos, or a hundred pounds. At thirty-three kilos, she was twelve kilos lighter than I, and yet she was three inches taller. (She'd gained height in the years we'd been writing to each other; I was stuck at my twelve-year-old stature, five feet two and a half inches.)

"I still don't want to gain weight, which I know is irrational, and my whole family is desperately concerned about me because like at 74 lbs. I'm a walking health hazard—the least germ caught could mean curtains—plus I may be doing permanent damage to myself, plus I look like a walking skeleton, but all this just doesn't make me able to see the light." She wrote that she was eating three good meals a day and a bedtime snack, so was metabolizing more or less normally. But depression continued to hit her hard from time to time, and occasionally she heard voices.

She wasn't able to keep the weight she'd gained. By September she'd dropped to sixty-eight pounds and once again needed hospitalization. This time she went to Texas, to a leading doctor in the field of eating disorders. Within six weeks she was up to ninety-seven pounds and also had gained, she wrote, "a lot of insight and resolve."

But that dissipated quickly once she left the protective environment of the hospital. Unable to stand her situation at home, she moved in with her older brother in Boston. She had found a therapist and a job as a nurse's aide in a convalescent home, but "was getting more and more depressed, and finally one night I overate, felt really suicidal, and ended up in the psych ward of Mt. Auburn Hospital for five weeks." She spent Christmas at her brother's on a day pass, and was discharged December 30.

Her first letter of 1975 came from a halfway house in the Boston suburb of Brookline. "There are 16 other residents, mostly in their 20s . . . sometimes it's a little lonely but I have made friends and it is getting better." The following weekend,

Joannie's mother would be driving up from New Jersey, bringing the beloved mice to keep her company.

She'd quit the depressing job in the convalescent home and was working at McDonalds, learning how to make milkshakes and operate a french-fry machine. She was also taking a course to become a guide at the New England Aquarium: "I can give you a good 3 minute talk on Priscilla the Octopus, or on sea anemones—care to try me?"

In September she started at Boston University as a biology major, writing that being back in school was "sort of rough but I have to at least make it through the year. . . ."

She made it only four months. "Boston University just got too big and impersonal" and living alone in her own apartment after the halfway house didn't help. By January she had re-enrolled at Rutgers. "Things are going fairly well; ups and downs as usual."

And so it went on, through 1976 and 1977—"ups and downs as usual" as Joannie struggled with demons I couldn't begin to fathom. I'd exhausted my repertoire of reassurance: I seemed to have been repeating the same platitudes for years.

Each time she wrote it seemed that she had a new major: horticulture in one letter, anthropology the next. She would send me the address of a new apartment she'd leased and I'd write to her there, only to be informed in her next letter that she'd never moved in. "I chickened out, stayed home instead which I know isn't a good situation . . . but I'm too afraid to leave."

For me, there had been no question of leaving home until I turned twenty-one—my parents just wouldn't consider it. But finally, in 1977, they decided I was old enough, at last, to move into my own apartment. I found a one-bedroom flat behind a dry-cleaning shop a few blocks from the university in Glebe, the neighborhood in which Darleen had predicted we'd both have a "little house" one day. It was a wonderful old neighborhood—a finger of land jutting into the harbor, with small workers' cottages and terrace houses pressed cozily together. My flat had a view of a park from the sitting room and a narrow, shady garden in back.

But I was moving there without Darleen. Instead of returning to Sydney, she'd been offered a job in a big advertising agency in Los Angeles. "It's all more competitive," she wrote to me just after she arrived there. "Business is worshipped like sports are at home. Everybody says—'oh, you're from Australia, what are you doing here, I've always wanted to go there.' It's too early to make statements about the place though. . . . I'm glad you liked the Matisse poster, I thought that was your favorite of his. Did I tell you that was the blue of the sky when we climbed Mount Baldy?" Her plan, she wrote, was to stay for just a year. But her life didn't go according to that plan. On her way back to Sydney she met a tall, charming Englishman. By the time I moved into my little flat in Glebe she had married him in London.

I hung the Matisse poster, *The Dance,* in my freshly decorated bedroom, and imagined her nodding approvingly. Trevor and a few of his architect friends had spent a weekend turning my flat into a designer version of student digs: stark white walls and stripped timbers, exposed standstock bricks and rush matting. It was Trevor's gift to me, to make up for the fact that he, too, was about to leave Australia for his Big Trip. He'd finally earned his degree after years of night classes, and he planned to go and see the architectural treasures of Europe, perfecting his French and his skiing en route. By then I was inured to departures. They were part of the price of being Australian. I knew I'd miss Trevor, but I had gained enough confidence to welcome some time as an unattached person again.

"It sounds as if life is treating you fairly decently!" wrote

Joannie that April. "Except for the guy who took off for Zermatt—that would be a real coincidence if your fellow met Dolfi in Zermatt. Dolfi works there on and off as a ski instructor—but he's in Switzerland, I'm here, and in answer to your question, my love life is zilch and 100% absolutely nothing. Partly it's me because I just don't feel ready to get involved with a guy at this point—my whole social life . . . has in the past two weeks been rather difficult, as has everything—well, it's just been a rotten two weeks."

Joannie's letters, mostly sad, would thud like a stone into the contented bustle of my new life. I would set each letter on my desk, resolving to answer it quickly. But it would get buried under the notes for some prolix paper on "Working-Class Politics" or "The Mannerist Esthetic of Michelangelo." It might be more than a month or two before I finally scribbled a guilty reply.

She always wrote back immediately. But her letters increasingly began with a gentle, jokey reproach for my neglect: "Dear Geraldine, Hi! I haven't heard from you in ages." "Dear Geraldine, Hi! Long time no hear (again)." "Dear Geraldine, Hi! I was really glad to finally hear from you. I was afraid you were swallowed up like Harold Holt!" [the Australian Prime Minister who disappeared while swimming in the surf].

As I settled into uni life, old friends had gradually fallen away, like old leaves making way for new ones at the change of season. I had no intention of shedding Joannie, but to write about my studies, which were going well, or my romances, which were agreeably diverting, seemed tactless when I knew that both those areas of her life were troubled.

Even food, so problematic to her, had become one of my greatest pleasures. Darleen had started me down the road to gourmet cooking back in 1966 when she decided that the two of us would make a special dinner to celebrate our parents' twentieth wedding anniversary. The centerpiece of the menu would be duck *à l'orange,* which would have been unremarkable, except that it was the first thing either of us had ever cooked. It was typical of Darleen's style: go directly to haute cuisine, do not pass hamburgers.

She sent Mum and Dad off to see the romantic French film, *A Man and a Woman,* while we tried to find the verb in recipe instructions such as "julienne orange zest" and puzzled over the meaning of "deglaze pan." Our pan was Teflon: it didn't have a glaze. Somehow, we figured that deglazing involved tossing in some brandy. We'd extinguished the inferno and hidden the evidence by the time our parents returned from the movie.

Later, working weekends as a waitress, I learned how to reduce a stock, how to fillet a fish, how to garnish a plate. I enrolled in cooking classes that were virtually free, thanks to government subsidies, and got to sample creations such as oysters *au champagne sabayon, boeuf carbonnade,* hay-roasted lamb with *hollandaise minceur* that were far beyond a student's budget.

By the time I moved into the Glebe apartment I knew how to turn cheap organ meats into succulent terrines and how to transform the bargains of a morning's trip to the nearby fish market into delicious meals. I found I could hide my shyness in the role of show-off chef, and the kitchen of my little flat became a favorite haunt of my uni peers. But these were pleasures that I didn't even dare to broach with Joannie. We were both using food to impose control on an uncertain social world. But my way was through feast and hers through famine.

Somehow, Joannie managed to stay in school through 1977, and it seemed as if we would finish our degrees within months of each other the following year. She was thinking about graduate school; I couldn't wait to get a job.

I wanted to be a reporter, and I'd laid siege to the largest daily paper, the *Sydney Morning Herald,* hoping to be one of the half dozen cadet journalists they hired every year. In February 1979, I started work as a cadet on the *Herald* sports desk.

Cadetship was a one-year purgatory designed to humble university graduates and teach them how to accurately handle reams of small facts. Of all the tasks—compiling the TV guide, monitoring the police radio scanner, writing up the shipping news, reading the sackloads of letters to the editor—the lot of the sports cadet was perhaps the most miserable.

The sports section occupied a pen in a corner of the newsroom, walled off by filing cabinets and gated by a pair of giant, mostly empty wastebaskets. To enter, one had to wade through the calf-deep deposits of trash that hadn't quite made it into the bins—tomato-sauce-stained meat-pie wrappers, sandwich crusts, coffee cups, cigarette butts, and mounds of crumpled 8-ply—the little booklets of paper interleaved with carbon on which stories were typed, a paragraph per booklet, in those pre-word-processor days.

The sports reporters themselves were a set of hard-drinking, chain-smoking clichés: all men, mostly middle-aged, largely dissipated. Even the few younger ones had incipient beer guts. The most wasted-looking of all were the half dozen racing writers, and these were the men for whom I was assigned to work. My arrival triggered an automatic, too-mindless-to-be-malicious fiesta of bottom-pinching sexual harassment that taught me to move through the section in a kind of sideways crab scuttle: the only way to keep my ass out of reach of roving hands.

The biggest part of my job was to compile the information these men needed in order to pick winners. "Doing the details," as the job was called, required going to every race meeting—gallops, trotting and, late on Saturday nights, that last resort of the hopeless punter, "the dogs." On big cardboard file cards, I had to keep detailed records of each runner: where it was at the turn, where at the finish, the condition of the track, the duration of each race, what the betting odds were early in the day, what they went out to, what they were at the race's start. The work was both mind-numbing and nerve-racking, since some country bookmakers paid out on the *Herald*'s results and an error could cost thousands.

What made it all worse was the compulsory drinking. I had to travel to and from the track with the racing writers, who always stopped off at the pub on the way back to the office. There, the tyranny of the "shout" meant that everybody was required to buy at least one round of drinks. With five reporters, that meant at least five beers had to be consumed to escape the ignominy of being branded "a gutless sheila who can't hold her piss" or, worse, "that stuck-up uni sheila who thinks she's too bloody good to down a beer with us." Buffering my nervousness at the university had already made me a fierce drinker: I kept frosted glasses in the refrigerator for the perfectly mixed martinis that lubricated my lingering social awkwardness. But the drinking of the sportswriters was a new league in which I had no desire to compete. When I left the pub, my grandest ambition was to make it upright to the huge gray *Herald* building rotating through space on the other side of the road.

It wasn't exactly the kind of world-changing reporting I'd imagined, and I lived for the day of the three-month assignment changeover, when I'd be sent to a paradise such as the letters page. When the assignments finally went up on the newsroom notice board and I saw that I'd been condemned to another three months in the sports section, I almost resigned on the spot.

To stay sane, I'd started writing unsolicited features for the paper's soft underbellies, the Home Section and the Weekend magazine. On the day one of these—a pensée about the Ice Age in my undefrosted freezer—appeared, I suddenly got a summons from the *Herald*'s editor-in-chief, otherwise known as

God. Nobody I knew had ever seen him. Omnipotent yet invisible, the editor-in-chief communicated only by memos. I'd had one of these on a previous story—a one-liner saying he'd found the piece "readable."

The summons to his office arrived just as I'd returned from an afternoon at the racetrack. I wasn't exactly dressed for success. Dust crusted my wind-blown hair, manure rimmed my sensible sneakers, and a dribble of meat-pie gravy and tomato sauce traveled in a Jackson Pollockesque splatter across the front of my dress. For fragrance, I was wearing that unmistakable eau-de-pub medley of stale tobacco and beer. In a panic, I rushed across the newsroom to the fashion section and threw myself on the mercy of the cadet assigned there. In the staff bathroom, she scrubbed me off, made me up and loaned me her high-heeled burgundy boots, in which I tottered off to meet God.

David Bowman had the face of a kindly boy, topped by a mop of prematurely silvered hair. After a brief comment on that day's article and a polite query on the state of my shorthand (cadets were supposed to reach a hundred words a minute before they could pass out of trainee status) he dismissed me. Relieved that I hadn't been sacked for muddling the odds on some greyhound, I left the office baffled as to why Captain Memo, as Bowman was also nicknamed, hadn't simply put it in writing.

The next morning the sports editor waved me into his cubicle. This gruff, taciturn man had barely said a word to me since I'd joined his section. He looked up over the heavy black rims of his glasses. "Want you round in features," he barked, and returned his attention to the pile of 8-ply on his desk.

And so I found myself vaulted into one of the best jobs on the paper, writing everything from celebrity profiles to investigations of toxic waste dumps. Suddenly I had a real salary and an office with art on the walls.

• • •

"We're starting a scholarship to send an Australian reporter to study at the Graduate School of Journalism at Columbia University in New York," David Bowman told me one day. The scholarship was being created to memorialize Greg Shackleton, a young reporter who had been killed by the Indonesian army while covering the invasion of East Timor. "I really think you should apply." This, I realized, might be my Big Trip. New York for a year would be perfect. And I would know someone there.

Joannie had been accepted to the Graduate School of Social Work at Rutgers and was living in an apartment in New Brunswick. "I do hope you get to study at Columbia," she wrote when I told her of my application, "it's a good school but as you said, we could finally get to meet each other!" Her weight remained low and her eating habits precarious, but she seemed at last to be winning the battle to normalize them. On weekends, I imagined the two of us wandering a museum in Manhattan, or going off together to watch the leaves change in Vermont.

In spite of the different turn our lives had taken as seventeen-year-olds, I still had more years of shared confidences with Joannie than with any of my mates in Sydney. There was no one left who remembered my Mr. Spock obsession or whose first adolescent stirrings of political consciousness had so closely paralleled my own. I had written things to Joannie that I hadn't divulged to anyone else. And she had exposed her fears to me in a way that no Australian friend had ever dared. I wouldn't need a martini before I visited Joannie: she would understand my shyness. I knew, I'd always known, that when we met each other we would be soul mates.

And so it seemed perfect to me that when I got the news that I'd won the scholarship, the second "Star Trek" movie was about to be released. "Don't you dare go see it until I get there!" I wrote.

She didn't answer at once, which I thought odd, since even a trivial "how are you" note always got an instant, enthusiastic response. But perhaps she was away, as she so often was in summer, in her cabin on Martha's Vineyard.

The letter in reply finally arrived at my parents' house in the last week of August, just as I was packing. A note on the front said: "Please forward to NYC if she has already left!"

It was from Joannie's mother, and it began with an apology for its lateness. "I am sorry, but far sorrier to say what I have to—that Joannie died unexpectedly . . . due apparently to some metabolic catastrophe, she just did not wake up one day."

Part Two

9

She Was
Going to Be You

⁓∾◍∾⁓

Late at night, when the babble of voices from the portside restaurant finally ebbs, different sounds flow up the hill. There is a gentle tinkling, then an answering note, deeper and more resonant. Ping-ting. Bong. Ping-ting. Bong.

Don't these phantom bell ringers ever rest? I toss on the narrow bed, unable to sleep. Finally, pulling the orange coverlet over my shoulders, I step out into the starry night. Down in the port, boats rock in their moorings, their shrouds gently clinking. Ping-ting. A pulse of white glare briefly illuminates the dark trail of my footsteps across the dew-wet grass. It is the beam from the Gay Head lighthouse. Somewhere out on the inky water a bell buoy chimes a further warning. Bong.

I wander back across the meadow to the cabin where my husband and son are sleeping. Joannie's cabin on Martha's Vineyard. It is 1996. She has been dead for fifteen years.

"The cabin is just a cabin," she wrote in August 1972, "one room, with two beds in it, which I took over two years ago and have since redecorated. Now it looks halfway presentable—I'm working on some new curtains for it now—and your mobile fits right in with everything else. Thanks!" I had sent her a mobile for her birthday that June, and she had brought it to the Vineyard for her redecoration project.

The strings on the mobile rotted years ago and the thing fell apart. I can't even remember what it looked like. But the curtains Joannie worked on in 1972—orange and yellow hippyish swirls—still hang in the windows. And the linoleum she chose, with its flower-power daisies, brightens the dark wood floor. An old piece of 1970s macramé dangles from a beam.

The summer of the redecoration was also the summer that Joannie decided she was too fat for her swimsuit. She had just turned seventeen: the year of the beginning of the end of her life.

And now I am here, as I was last year. Joannie's echo.

"I'm terribly pleased at your winning the scholarship and coming to New York," Joannie's mother Elizabeth had written to me in 1982, when she broke the news of Joannie's death. "You must get in touch with us and come to visit—even stay a while if you need a place."

But I did not get in touch, although I thought about it almost every week of the nine lonely months I spent in New York City. Even after three years as a reporter, cold-calling strangers and doorstopping politicians, I remained excruciatingly shy in my personal life. When it came to making contact with Joannie's family, I couldn't summon the nerve to pick up the phone.

That autumn at Columbia University, I began to glimpse for the first time the sources of Joannie's despair. Growing up had been so easy in Sydney, where childhood passed at its own leisurely pace, with no rush into adulthood.

At Columbia, I came to see the different way achievement was measured for my American classmates. For them, graduate school wasn't the surprising and luxurious blessing it was for me. Instead, it was just another hurdle on a track determined for them at birth. And for many of them, the bar was always set just a hair beyond the point that they could comfortably reach.

I'd been spared the pressure that my American contemporaries felt, some of them since preschool. For me, with parents who'd never had a chance to go to college, any academic achievement was treated as a small miracle. If my grade in a subject was a credit or a distinction, that was great and we celebrated. No one asked me why I hadn't got a high distinction.

Within a month or two I'd moved out of the grungy student residence hall within earshot of sporadic gunfire in Morningside Park. I'd heard of a room in an apartment tucked above a diner that sounded like my old place near the uni in Sydney. I would be sharing with a vivacious woman named Valerie, about three years younger than I, who was dating an Australian reporter.

I soon learned that she was dating a great many other people as well. Valerie worked days as a bookkeeper and was usually asleep in her room at the far end of our railroad apartment when I returned from class in the early evening. At 1 A.M., when I'd gone to bed, she would get up and dress for her night's entertainment. I would catch a sleepy glimpse of her as she headed out the door. Her taste in clothes ran to tight leather and microscopic mini-skirts; in clubs, to places with names like Hellfire; in men, from rough trade to the sexually ambiguous.

One night she arrived home at 5 A.M. and disappeared giggling into her bedroom with a uniformed police officer. When I asked her about him, she tossed her head and howled with laughter. "Oh no, honey, he ain't a cop. He's just, like, really into authority. He has these neat handcuffs."

A few weeks later, when the real police called, looking for one of Valerie's regulars, a man named Sticks who was wanted in connection with a murder in a gay bar, I decided it was time to move out. Kate, one of my best friends from high school, had come to New York to study acting. She had a room available in an apartment in the East Village.

Moving in with Kate was a relief. My Sydney childhood—even my Sydney adulthood—hadn't quite prepared me for Valerie. In the staid suburbs of Sydney there had been no need to feign sophistication and, in a cloistered all-girls school, no rush to be sexy. But in New York it seemed that everything from sitcoms to sermons assumed a world in which nine-year-olds had opposite-sex admirers, thirteen-year-olds went out on dates and fifteen-year-olds had sex. I'd hated my parents' strictness about curfews and living on my own because it was holding me back from the adult passions I craved. But in New York I began to wonder if that wasn't preferable to what had happened to my American friends, who seemed to have had adult passions thrust at them. They'd been forced into bloom like branches of hothouse blossoms.

Our extended timetable for growing up had saved me from plunging too soon into an emotional deep end where I might not have been able to find my footing. I began to wonder if Joannie had felt rushed out of her childhood. I knew that one theory of anorexia suggests that young women strive to stay thin as a way to hold on to their girlishness, starving so their bodies won't ripen into the rounded curves of womanhood. Joannie had written of her reluctance to accept adult responsibility, and her frequent flights home to the nest suggested her unease with the adult world of independence. But it wasn't until I lived in New York that I understood the different meanings that "womanhood" and "adult" had for the two of us. For the first, time, I could see what it was that had terrified her so.

As fall turned to winter in Manhattan, I did the things I'd imagined doing with Joannie—made weekend sorties to see the leaves turn, wandered museums on snowy Sundays. But I never went to the second "Star Trek" movie. I just couldn't bring myself to see it without her.

Somewhere toward the end of the academic year, I began to have glimpses of the possibility of an alternative life—an American life—different from the one that was waiting for me back in Sydney. Chance encounters turned to job offers. And then I met a fellow student with blond curls and a history as a labor organizer among poor black woodcutters in Mississippi. As a kid, Tony had watched "Star Trek" in his family's rambling Victorian house in a suburb just like Maplewood. Summers, he roamed around Cape Cod and Martha's Vineyard.

He should have met Joannie, not me. And it was she who should have been stepping through the professional doors that were opening for me. By spring, I began to have the eerie sensation that I had slipped into Joannie's place and was leading the life she should have had.

The following summer, just a few months before Tony and I were married, he took me to Martha's Vineyard. We went to watch the sunset at Menemsha—the place that for so many years had been a postmark I didn't know how to pronounce. We sat on the beach and watched the sky turn purple and gold—the colors on the postcards Joannie had sent me. As the sun dropped into the ocean, I imagined her sitting there in my place, happy and in love.

I was lonely for her. I looked up the hill to the collection of fishing shacks and holiday homes behind us, and wondered which of them had been hers. That night, back at the little inn where we were staying, I pulled out the skinny Vineyard phone book. Her family's name was there—the only listing under that name on the island. At last I screwed up my courage and dialed. I sat there on the bed as the phone rang, and rang, echoing into the emptiness of a summer home already deserted for the year.

· · ·

It was nine more years before I finally contacted Joannie's mother. After Columbia, I went to Cleveland to take a job in *The Wall Street Journal*'s news bureau there. The year after that, Tony and I married in France. We spent the next eight years in Sydney, Cairo and London, living out of the never quite un-packed duffel bags of Foreign Correspondents.

When we returned to the United States in 1993, Tony longed to revisit the Vineyard. For me, the place was still haunted by Joannie. Every time I sat laughing over a delicious meal, I thought of her, and how she should have been there, enjoying it in my place. And then of the long years in which she'd been unable to enjoy such meals, and of the many ways, during those years, that I'd failed her as a correspondent, and as a friend.

Before my resolve failed again, I wrote to the old address in Maplewood.

On the phone, Joannie's mother had a strong New Englander's voice that broke as we talked of her daughter. "I was very touched to get your letter," she said. "Come and see me. I can't talk any more now."

And so, on a beautiful fall day in 1993, as a crisp breeze pushed little cumulus clouds around on the horizon, the conduc-tor handed back my yellow ticket with the long list of New Jersey suburbs. The hole punched through Maplewood made it official: I was finally making the journey I'd thought about for so long. The train rattled past Newark's razor-wired demolition sites and graffiti-scrawled gas-storage tanks, then through hum-ble neighborhoods of simple working-class houses. Eventually, about twenty miles southwest of Manhattan, trees closed in, offering only glimpses of the winding boulevards and elegant homes beyond.

Joannie's house was exactly as I had imagined it: a charming

Victorian surrounded by trees. On the porch steps her cat, Selena, an old lady in the reckoning of cat years, stretched on the warm stone. Upstairs, her bedroom had been kept as it was: a pretty room of nooks and windows, flooded with sunlight, the green plants she tended still thriving under her mother's care. In a brilliantly lit window alcove stood her desk—her writing desk.

I imagined her there, in late August 1968—a just-turned thirteen-year-old, tanned from a summer at the beach. Hiding her shyness behind a flimsy airmail sheet, she wrote: "I'd like to be your pen-pal. I have several others in Austria. People often confuse Austria with Australia. They'll ask me why I can speak German, or why I've got a slight European accent, and I'll answer that I spent some time in Austria. Then, they will say brightly, 'Oh, did you see any kangaroos there?' "

Downstairs, at the breakfast bar in the kitchen, Joannie's mother Elizabeth served me tea and homemade cake, and we began the conversation that we would continue for years, off and on, changing the subject when it became too painful to continue. The subject, of course, was Joannie.

That afternoon we filled yawning gaps in my knowledge of the family, driving stakes through the heart of my fevered adolescent fantasies. Joannie's parents were CIO, not CIA: they met at a Congress of Industrial Organizations conference. Before her marriage, Elizabeth worked for John Lewis, the legendary trade unionist and CIO leader. Later she taught poetry and became chair of a state college English department. Joannie's father was an English professor. They were in Austria as Fulbrights, not spies. Joannie's left-wing views were part of the family consensus, not a source of friction.

According to Elizabeth, Joannie's conflicts with her father were of the common or garden variety: he was demanding, especially academically—"it was a real blot on the escutcheon to get a low grade"—and he was puritanical about relations with the opposite sex. These areas of friction were exacerbated by his day-to-day distance. Forty-six years old when Joannie was born, he was preoccupied with his teaching and research. So Joannie lived mostly in her mother's orbit, a close relationship that sounded just like the one I'd had with my mother.

Joannie's father had died earlier that year. If I had left it any longer to write, I would not have found Elizabeth in Maplewood. The house was for sale, and she planned to move to a retirement community in another state. She had started the chore of packing up a lifetime's memories. "It's so hard to throw anything away," she said. Especially anything of Joannie's.

I had an evening plane to catch from Newark airport. I was on the steps, heading for my cab, when Elizabeth disappeared into the kitchen and returned with an apple. "In case you get hungry on the plane," she said, tucking it in the pocket of my coat. It was exactly the kind of thing my mother would do.

The Martha's Vineyard house "has a kitchen, a living room, a dining room, a bedroom, a study with a bed in it, plus couches in various places that convert to beds," Joannie wrote in 1972. It had been built a hundred years earlier as a fisherman's cottage. Her uncle had bought it as a writer's retreat. His books still lined the walls of the cabin—faded hardbacks titled *Mission to Moscow* by Joseph E. Davies or *The Un-Americans* by Frank J. Donne. Because he used the small barn by the house as a place to produce a left-wing magazine, the knoll on which it sat, just behind Dutcher Dock, had become known locally as Socialist Hill. Joannie's father inherited the property on his brother's death in 1968. Now, with the surrounding cottages rented out for ten thousand dollars a month to summer vacationers, the name "Socialist Hill" is one of those local oddities inscrutable to all but old-timers.

Over the years, the winding track up from the port has

carved its way closer and closer to the house, until the tiny front porch almost seems to topple into the roadway. When Joannie's mother rises from her rocking chair to greet me, her white hair almost brushes the low porch ceiling. At eighty, she is tall and straight as a poplar.

When I visit Elizabeth on Martha's Vineyard, there is always a fresh-baked pie cooling on the counter of the cabin's tiny, dollhouse kitchen. Something wholesome and good—fresh-picked corn or new potatoes, the local farmer's broccoli or ruby-red tomatoes—waits to be prepared for dinner.

Elizabeth vividly remembers when Joannie became picky about such meals. "She had a friend staying with her that summer and they marched into the kitchen together one day and announced they were going to go on a diet," she says. "I laughed. Everyone was going on a diet at that time."

We take our coffee out into the neat little garden between the house and the cabin. Bright-faced cosmos bob in the breeze; Elizabeth made a special trip in June to plant annuals so that the garden would bloom through the month of August, when the family comes. All the children visit—Jack, the onetime conscientious objector, now an electrical engineer in Santa Fe; Jamie, Joannie's older sister from Berkeley, who takes pictures and works on archeological digs; Joel, the biochemist, a cancer researcher in Buffalo. And now, as August draws to a close, I have come, with my husband and new baby. We bathe him on the kitchen table in an old plastic tub that has seen service as baby bath for Elizabeth's grandchildren. And at night, sleeping in the cabin where Joannie should be sleeping, I'm overwhelmed again with the feeling that I am having her life.

Sitting in banana chairs as our damp swimsuits flap on the clothesline, Elizabeth explains one of Joannie's failed attempts to get her own apartment in Boston while she went to university there. "She was going to BU, at the time," is what Elizabeth

says. But what I hear is: "She was going to be you, at the time."
She was going to be me, at the time—content in my little flat in
Glebe, Sydney, heading happily toward career, marriage, family.

But, of course, she wasn't going to be me at all.

When Joannie returned to Maplewood with her parents in the
fall of 1972, it took three months for anyone to acknowledge that
the summer diet had gone too far. "I noticed she was eating less,
but she was also wearing loose clothes, so I hadn't realized the
extent of it," Elizabeth says. "I *had* been concerned that she
seemed to be withdrawing again."

As a child and young teenager, Joannie had been painfully
shy. For Halloween, she would dress up as Mr. Spock. "In the
costume—with the pointed ears and so on—she looked just like
him. But even without it, she was so perfect at imitating him, it
concerned me—that affectless expression—it seemed part of her
extreme withdrawal. It worried me, but I thought, 'I was shy
too: I got over it.'"

Elizabeth had been relieved when Joannie, in her junior
year, burst from her cocoon to run for class president, win parts
in local plays. Then, in early summer, she went off to Salzburg
to the American Institute for Foreign Study. Something happened there. She had written to me that the program wasn't
what she'd hoped for, and that she was "eating far too much."
Elizabeth knows that Joannie was extremely lonely, but beyond
that, she isn't sure what went wrong. She only knows that the
daughter who came home wasn't the emerging butterfly who
left.

It was just before Thanksgiving when Joannie confided to
her mother that her diet was out of control. The next day the
two of them went to the family doctor. "When I saw her
stripped, I was appalled. The doctor said she must be anorectic,
and I said, 'What's that?'"

The late August sunshine is strong, but that isn't the reason Elizabeth shades her eyes with a long-fingered hand. Now, she knows as much as any lay person about anorexia. She has read all the textbooks, all the scholarly articles. She knows that anorectics tend to come predominantly from higher-social-class families, that their parents are described as overprotective, over-concerned and overambitious; that the typical anorectic's family is dominated by the mother, with the father an emotional absentee.

Elizabeth was forty when Joannie was born, at a time when giving birth at forty was far less common than it is now. Everyone assumed the pregnancy was accidental. "It wasn't. She was wanted."

Over the years Elizabeth has had plenty of time to reflect on whether the gap in their ages caused problems, and to examine minutely every facet of her mothering. "Sometimes, when I read about the role of the anorectic's mother, I see some of my traits described there. But I also see some that are not mine at all."

Joannie's troubled relationship with her father hadn't seemed any worse than the usual frictions between a strict parent and a child entering adulthood. The irrationality of her anorectic behavior—insisting on making elaborate, rich meals, then refusing to eat them, exercising compulsively despite her skeletal frailness—aggravated her father intensely. "I know it hurt him, when she chose to take my name and abandon his," Elizabeth says. It took years before "he realized that the things that got on his nerves were part of her illness, and he became more loving and pliable." Joannie had written to me, toward the end, that she and her father were getting along better, "and that's nice." By then, she had resumed using his surname.

But there was one other way in which she had rejected him. Both Joannie and I, as girls, had thrown ourselves into obsessive interests. Talking about this trait with Elizabeth, I mention that my Mr. Spock mania had been replaced by an absorption with Israel and Jews. I tell Elizabeth how I'd hoped that Joannie might be Jewish, or at least share my fascination, and how disappointed I'd been when she'd dismissed my outpourings on the subject with a few uninterested sentences.

Elizabeth's eyes widen. "Joannie never told you that her father was Jewish?"

After the family doctor diagnosed her anorexia, Joannie told him she was anxious about the approach of Thanksgiving, with its compulsory feasting. "He said, 'Just relax and let your mother make you a turkey sandwich,' " Elizabeth recalls.

But Joannie couldn't relax. She couldn't sleep. Her refusal to eat and her exhausted state convinced her parents that she needed hospitalization. But Joannie became distraught at the suggestion. They gave her Thorazine to calm her. "We must have given her too much," Elizabeth says, because by the time they arrived at the emergency room her blood pressure had plummeted. Joannie was admitted for the months-long treatment about which she'd written to me in early 1973.

And so the pattern began that would continue for the next eight years. Joannie thrived in the protected environment of the hospital, gained weight and pulled out of depression. But with each release came relapse. Elizabeth remembered getting Joannie ready to go to Vassar—making the Indian-print bedspread and curtains for the single room she'd wanted, but had written to me that she disliked and found too lonely. "Her balance was precarious—the hope was that she'd find herself if everything went perfectly."

But it didn't. And on a weekend trip home she binged, felt guilty and took the overdose of antidepressant she'd written about in her letter of November 1973. She told her parents she'd taken the Tofranil. They rushed her to the bathroom and induced vomiting. Elizabeth was stunned by the amount of food that came up—the magnitude of the binge. Because she'd vomited so much, they thought she'd surely eliminated the drug from her system. "She went to take a nap, and then I couldn't wake her up," Elizabeth recalls. And so began the nightmare weeks of emergency room, followed by intensive care, coronary care and psychiatric hospital again.

Joannie realized that she wasn't psychologically strong enough for Vassar, but the fact that she couldn't go back threw her into despair. For weeks, Elizabeth said, "She'd just sit with her head in her hands."

Determined to find the best therapist, the family searched out Hilde Bruch, the eating-disorders specialist in Texas. She remembers the relief with which she left Joannie in Dr. Bruch's care, feeling that for once she would be safe. Joannie did so well that Elizabeth urged her to stay on in Texas and enroll in university there, so that she could remain close to the therapist. But Joannie chose to come home. Once back, "all the old stresses and temptations" seized her again.

In her long search for answers, Elizabeth has wondered if Joannie's voices and fears indicated a schizophrenia-like disorder. She feels reasonably sure that fear of growing up and unease with emerging sexuality were a large part of the problem.

Joannie had been just sixteen in the summer of 1971, when she became involved with Dolfi in Switzerland. ("He's what I guess would be called my summer boyfriend," she had written to me when she went back to visit him the following year, "and would be my winter boyfriend too, if only possible!") But it wasn't possible, and so back in Maplewood there was another boy, and a relationship that ended in his rejection of her. That rebuff seemed to speed her withdrawal. "I often think that if she'd just been able to be with Dolfi it would have been all right," Elizabeth says. "He had the sensitivity that was needed to deal with her sexual fears."

Joannie last saw Dolfi just after her graduation, when she was well enough to take a trip to Europe. The reunion was warm, and may have helped her as she gathered herself together to apply for graduate school. Once, she had written to Dolfi's mother about her pleasure in tending plants, and his mother had written back, saying, "Someday you will tend people." In the study of social work, Joannie at last seemed to have found a way to subsume her own problems by looking for solutions to the problems of others. She also had an excellent new therapist and was eating much more normally. "She seemed at last to be winning the battle," Elizabeth says. But Elizabeth also knew the dangers of too much optimism. Joannie had been active in the Anorexia Aid Society, writing for its journal. "She wrote a couple of articles that said she'd recovered," says Elizabeth. "I'd cross my fingers because I could see it was not secure."

Joannie moved into the apartment in New Brunswick and called her mother to ask advice about how to defrost the refrigerator. The next day she called again. She had misplaced the phone number of her therapist. "She said she needed to talk to her because she was anxious about a statistics course." As Elizabeth put down the phone, the familiar fears for her daughter returned. Joannie was still rail-thin, and Elizabeth knew very well how easily an anxiety attack could trigger a dangerous eating episode.

The next day Joannie was found dead. The autopsy couldn't say whether the direct cause was heart arrhythmia brought on by an electrolyte imbalance, or aspiration of vomit. The years of near starvation had taken a terrible toll on all of her organs, and that last binge was one insult more than her frail body could bear.

· · ·

"We are still trying to recover our balance," Elizabeth had written to me back in 1982 when she broke the news of Joannie's death. Fifteen years later, she still is trying.

Joannie never wrote to tell me that she had become a Catholic in her final years, adopting the religion I'd cast aside. Hers was the Catholicism of the liberation theologians and the social-activist Maryknolls, very different from the rigid, conservative Church I'd known. Elizabeth had been drawn to the caring nuns and priests who had tried to help Joannie. After Joannie died, Elizabeth too had converted. And in the taking of the Eucharist she found a connection with her daughter.

But the questions have never stopped. Even after all the therapists and discussion groups and social workers, there remains no answer to the question of why Joannie became ill, or why, after she came so close, recovery in the end eluded her.

A relative of Joannie's who is a psychiatric pharmacologist at Yale believes Joannie suffered an imbalance in her brain chemistry during the multiple hormonal changes of adolescence.

But Elizabeth is sure that "something much deeper than chemicals" was involved. She asks if I know the story of "The Snow Queen" by Hans Christian Andersen. When the Snow Queen tosses a piece of ice, it lodges in a little boy's heart and freezes it. He can no longer feel love. In the fairy tale, a little girl named Gerda searches the world for the boy and, when she finds him, her love melts the ice.

"Joannie's heart was frozen," Elizabeth says. "She was always trying desperately to warm it. But for Joannie no love was warm enough."

Alongside the tall stack of letters from my fifteen-year correspondence with Joannie there is a smaller, still growing pile that bears a similar handwriting. There are postcards from Menemsha, and letter-cards sold for the benefit of UNICEF or Catholic Relief Services or the League of Women Voters.

Elizabeth and I write to each other now. Her latest card has a pen-and-ink sketch of a Martha's Vineyard townscape. "We had a brief thunderstorm a couple of days after you left, when the sky was spectacular—it seemed feathered with the soft gray breasts of countless doves."

Elizabeth's letters are a link with that other, long-ago correspondence. But they have become much more than that. "I suspect you realize how much your visits mean," she writes in her latest letter, "because of course in my mind I've adopted you. How could it be otherwise?"

And in my mind I've adopted her. How could it be otherwise?

She was going to be you.

Joannie wasn't going to be me. But I'm grateful for the ways in which my life has allowed me to be her.

10

Arab,
Jew and Aussie

❧

1. contact book (purged?)
2. passport & visa
3. $ + local currency + Amex
4. notebooks & pens
5. shortwave + extension aerial + batteries
6. Pocket Flight Guide
7. sunglasses, sunscreen, hat
8. ½ doz. passport photos
9. ref. books + notes + novel
10. maps
11. canteen + water-purify tabs?
12. dried food?
13. pocket knife?
14. antibiotics, field dressings, hypodermic
15. deodorant, moisturizer, lipbalm, Handiwipes, Evian, hairbrush, tampons, toothbrush & paste
16. underpants and bra

17. long skirt, 2 khaki pants & vest, 2 long-sleeve shirts, 2 T-shirts, sneakers
18. king suit, pumps & stockings
19. chador?
20. BP vest?

For eight years this twenty-point checklist sat in a drawer of my bedside table, ready for the late night calls: "Saddam's gassed the Kurds." "Khomeini's finally kicked it."

Everything on the list, except item 20—the bulletproof vest—could be crammed into a nylon duffel bag that just fit under an airplane seat. (The first rule of Foreign Correspondence: never check in any luggage. It's unfortunate to arrive at an Arab summit in Casablanca only to find that your underwear is touring sub-Saharan Africa without you.) It took me about a year to fine-tune the list. It was the *New York Times*'s uncombed correspondent John Kifner who taught me to pack what he called a "king suit," even if the assignment I'd set out on didn't seem likely to call for a visit to royalty. You never knew when the local dictator might invite you to tea. Kifner also advised making space for a fat novel. Most assignments didn't leave a spare minute for recreational reading. But some (anything that involved waiting for an interview with Yasir Arafat or a plane out of Khartoum) could provide enough time to get through Proust.

Other lessons came from experience. Iraqi secret police riffling through my contact book showed me the wisdom of purging the names and numbers of local dissidents. And the words "Don't leave home without it" took on new meaning the day I found myself miming "tampon" to a Farsi-speaking pharmacy clerk in Iran.

• • •

Covering the racetrack in Sydney, or writing about the decline of basic industry in the American Midwest, I'd never imagined myself as someone whose packing list would include a chador, much less a bulletproof vest. After a year and a half with *The Wall Street Journal* in Cleveland, I'd gone home to Sydney, to get on with what I still thought of as my real life, my Australian life. But then the *Journal* decided it needed an Australasian bureau, and so I became a Foreign Correspondent who wasn't foreign, writing features about things that were familiar to me yet exotic to my readers. Since the *Journal* didn't have a pressing interest in hard news from Australia, I was free to write pretty much what I liked. In between corporate stories I'd roam the Outback for weeks at a time, profiling a bargeman who delivered supplies to remote Aboriginal settlements in the Northern Territory, or saddling up with one of the last of the Queensland cattle drovers.

In 1987, I'd just filed a piece on how New Zealand scientists were using the country's vast population of methane-producing, flatulent sheep to study global warming when the *Journal*'s foreign desk in New York called. New York never called me. On the foreign editor's international priorities list, Sydney rated a notch or two ahead of Djiboutiville. As I answered the phone, I worried she was calling to chastise me about too many tasteless sheep-fart jokes.

Instead, she was offering me one of the paper's plum jobs: Middle East correspondent covering a beat that ranged over twenty-two countries. The job had become vacant because its previous occupant decided to return to Washington after spending several days in an Iranian jail. The Iranians had accused him of being a Zionist spy. The *Journal* got him released after pointing out that he wasn't even Jewish.

One small problem about me replacing him: I was.

. . .

Three years earlier, on a wintry day in Cleveland, I had stepped into a tiled tub of purified rainwater, sunk to my knees and let the liquid close over me. Looking up at the blurred yellow shapes thrown against the tiled walls by the electric light, I exhaled and watched my last breath as a Gentile bubble upward.

I broke the surface, the water sluicing off my bare skin in sparkling cascades, and proclaimed the Shema—"Hear, O Israel, the Lord our God. The Lord is One." Tradition teaches that a convert is a Jewish soul trapped by mistake in a Gentile body. Immersion in the ritual bath frees the soul again. Perhaps that trapped soul explained why, fourteen years earlier, a Sydney girl who had never met a Jew walked around with a Star of David dangling against the collar of her Catholic-school uniform.

Daddy, back home in Sydney, had been delighted when I wrote to say that the romance with Tony seemed serious. "So fascinating to think we might have a genuine Jew boy in the family," he wrote. "I suspect it's in the genes somewhere." When he was a soldier in Palestine, he had fallen for a young sabra. She had ended the relationship because he wasn't Jewish.

Tony didn't care if I was Jewish or not, and seemed bemused when I announced I wanted to convert. The night of my mikvah, he came reluctantly to hear me read my Torah portion, dragging himself through the synagogue door burdened by the same childhood memories of boredom and dread that dogged me every time I had to enter a Catholic church.

I was trying to fill what Salman Rushdie has described as the religion-shaped hole in modern lives: a place that yearns for links with past communities and for a coherent reason to do the right thing rather than the expedient one. Now my links were with Tony's three-thousand-year-old Jewish heritage, a heritage that had always insisted that religion passes to the child through the mother. Unless I converted, our children wouldn't be Jews. Somehow, Tony's forebears had kept their tradition alive through the Babylonian exile, the Spanish Inquisition, Russia's pogroms, the Holocaust. I didn't want to be the one to bring it to an end.

And so on that frozen Midwestern morning I became a Jew. In a few weeks more I became a Jewish bride. Barely four years later I finally arrived in Israel.

My life had given me the teenage fantasy I'd cooked up as I wrote to my Israeli pen pals and dug my mother's vegetable garden pretending it was an embattled kibbutz. But it was my fantasy revised beyond recognition. When I arrived in Eretz Israel in December 1987, it wasn't as a swamp-draining Zionist pioneer but as a Foreign Correspondent with a reservation at the Jerusalem Hilton.

I was there to cover the eruption of rage that would become known as the intifada. Within a day of my arrival I found myself in the no man's land between Palestinian rocks and Israeli rubber bullets. I'd made a classic rookie-correspondent error, a colleague told me over drinks at the bar later that night. In an uprising or a war, you reduce your risk of getting hurt by half if you get behind one group of combatants. "Never get in the middle," he said. "You have to choose your side."

But what was my side? My colleague was talking of physical placement, but his words hummed with the internal dilemma I'd faced ever since my arrival. I'd become a Jew out of sentimental identification with the world's eternal underdogs, but the place in which I had arrived wasn't my father's tiny, defenseless little Israel, encircled by enemies. It was a tough state, using an army to put down civilian unrest. I had become a Jew because I wanted to be on my husband's side in the world. But in the streets of the occupied territories in the winter of 1987 that side was no longer an unambiguous place to be.

As I reported the course of the intifada, I found myself

making friends with both Arabs and Jews. But the relationships were always strained. The Palestinians demonized Israelis, the Israelis dehumanized Palestinians. On each side it was rare to find a shred of empathy for the other.

On the phone to Australia, conversations with my father were equally tiring. The enthusiasm he'd shared with me, that had given us some common ground, was now a place of prickly disagreement. His Zionism had hardened over the years into a faith that brooked none of the ambiguity that troubled me. He was as ardent as any West Bank settler, and kept up a steady stream of letters to the Sydney newspapers espousing the rightness of a tough Israeli response to the Palestinians.

I had been covering the intifada for a year when Arafat decided to make a symbolic Declaration of Independence for the occupied territories, to boost the young stone throwers' flagging morale. On the day of the announcement, the Israeli army deployed, to leave Palestinians in no doubt as to who controlled their "independent" land. The army declared the entire West Bank a closed military area. But soldiers couldn't block every shepherd's path, so early in the morning I crammed into the back of a rattling old Fiat with a group of Palestinian students. We bumped over a rocky trail through olive groves to the Arab town of Ramallah, joining a steady trickle of illicit traffic as we reached the edge of the city.

In Ramallah, soldiers were everywhere, ordering anyone on the street to go to their houses. They were on us within minutes, eighteen-year-olds much the same age as the Palestinian students, poking the muzzles of their assault rifles in our faces and yelling in Hebrew for our IDs. I pulled out my Australian passport and handed it over. The Israeli youths stared at it and then called for their officer.

He was in his thirties. From his slight paunch, it was obvious he was a reservist, called up for his compulsory month of annual duty. The fatigue of bad nights on unfamiliar army cots was etched into his face. He paged through the passport, eying the array of Arab visas. He raised his head and looked at me wearily. "I think you're a journalist, and I think you shouldn't be here." I didn't want to lie, but I didn't want to be escorted back to Jerusalem, either. "I'm just here with my friends," I said. "Just visiting."

We gazed at each other and recognized a kind of kinship. Both of us were in this tense West Bank town because of our jobs, jobs that demanded we do things that made us uncomfortable. "Get off the street," he said. "If I see you again I'll arrest you."

As I melted away with the students, I found myself thinking of my old pen pal Cohen. The reservist with the tousled hair and the softening midriff could be him, doing his annual military service. I tried to conjure a picture of Cohen from his letters to me so long ago. I wanted to find him, to turn up at his door and say, "See? Here I am. I told you I would come." Maybe military service had already claimed him, in the Yom Kippur War or in Lebanon. I wanted to find Mishal, too, and try out my newly acquired Arabic on him. But I hadn't written to either of them since the early 1970s.

And I had no time. With the Iran-Iraq War edging into an eighth year, Islamic fundamentalism on the rise, Lebanon in flames, price riots in Jordan and famine in the Horn of Africa, I was on the Frequent Flyer program from hell. More than a year into my new assignment, I hadn't taken a single day off. I could hardly spare the time to search for my old pen pals, even if I had a place to start.

I couldn't remember their old addresses. I supposed that their letters were lost, tossed out with school exercise books and birthday cards in some long-ago cleanup. It was five years before I found them in my father's neglected tea chests. And it was another two years before I set out to discover what had become of the teenagers who once lived in those faraway places.

• • •

"What is the purpose of your visit to Israel? Do you know anyone there? How do you know them? What are their names?"

The rapid-fire interrogations droned on. As I waited in line to be questioned by the El Al airlines security staff, I pulled the fragile old envelopes from my bag and studied the addresses. In a corner of my ticket envelope I clumsily doodled a fiery-looking Hebrew *alef,* trying to picture what Amme Street would look like on a Hebrew-lettered street sign. I practiced asking, *wayn is-sharia hatha?* (Where is this street?) in my rusty Arabic.

The people on line for the flight covered the spectrum of American Jewry. There were stylish Orthodox women from the Upper East Side, fulfilling the modest dress code of their faith with straw hats and long linen dresses; black-coated Hasidic men from Crown Heights; huge tour groups with towers of luggage, and Walkman-wearing teenagers off for their year abroad at Hebrew University. The tall, beefy youths jostled each other with the easy physicality of puppies. I wondered what their fellow students would make of them. Israelis go to university only after army service. I had seen them on campus: lean, self-contained, slow to smile, their faces prematurely lined and their watchful eyes grave.

All the passengers ahead of me had simple answers for the security checkers. But what *was* the purpose of my visit to Israel? I'd answered the question dozens of times before, drenched in sweat in the stifling old terminal of Cairo's international airport or shivering in the chilly expanse of London's Heathrow, waiting for flights that left late at night, the terminals empty and the halls patrolled by machine-gun-toting Egyptian soldiers or bulletproof-vested British police holding German shepherds on tight leashes. On those trips I'd always had press credentials and a clear assignment.

But this time all I had was a handful of old letters and a whim. The purpose of my visit to Israel was to find an Arab and a Jew I hadn't been in touch with in twenty-three years. I wanted to know how they had been treated by the history I had helped to write every day when I was a Foreign Correspondent. But I also wanted to get back in touch with that other foreign correspondent—the passionate young girl in faraway Sydney who dreamed of adventures in dangerous places, and then went on to have more adventures than she'd ever imagined.

"And what is the purpose of your visit to Israel?" As I tried to answer, the grim young El Al interrogator peered at the letters. The old-fashioned design of the stamps intrigued her: they'd been issued before she was born. She called over the flight's security chief, a wary man who questioned me closely. Finally he handed back the letters as the young woman marked my boarding pass with the sticker that would allow me to board the flight. Their stern faces softened into sudden smiles. "We think it is a very beautiful story," she said. "We wish you luck."

Hours later I woke from a cramped doze as the plane banked over Tel Aviv. Below, an edge of brilliant blue sea sparkled against the gray concrete sprawl of the city. Along the coastline, solar panels glinted from the rooftops of boxy apartments. An Israeli writer once observed that he preferred the unhandsome chaos of jerry-built Tel Aviv to the ancient gleaming stone of Jerusalem. Jerusalem, he complained, was too holy and too demanding. "If I forget Tel Aviv," he said, "my tongue won't cleave to the roof of my mouth."

I wondered if there was an Israeli Sam Spade down there somewhere in a dingy office who would help me with my search if I got desperate. To find Cohen, I knew I could try the army: almost all Israelis are soldiers, and the army has to know how to find them quickly in time of war. In Nazareth, I had a journalist friend on the Arabic paper. I was sure he would have some ideas about how to locate Mishal.

But first I would go to the old addresses, no matter how unlikely it was that the trail would be fresh enough to follow after twenty-three years. In that time I had moved house fifteen times and wound up ten thousand miles from where I started. If any of my old pen pals presented themselves at the door of the house they'd written to in Concord, my trail would be colder than a frosted beer glass at the corner pub.

It was dusk when I pulled off the coastal highway and drove into a small town on Israel's narrow waistline north of Tel Aviv. Cohen's home town was once a *moshav*—a farming co-op in which families worked their own land, sharing machinery and marketing crops jointly. Over time, the *moshav* had been swamped by the sprawl reaching out from Tel Aviv and had grown into a residential community of some 7,000. Now only a few melon fields and orange groves remained.

It was that Mediterranean hour when the heat has finally eased and the heavy shutters have been flung open. People walked their dogs past neat little bungalows with bougainvillea-splashed gardens and mango trees. I pulled over near two smiling women gossiping on the street corner. One of them was pushing her sleeping baby in a kibbutz-designed crib on wheels that allows parents to take slumbering infants with them to the communal dining hall. I showed the women the old mauve envelope with the Amme Street address on it, written awkwardly in a hand unpracticed in the Roman alphabet. They puzzled over the street name. Neither had ever heard of it, which was odd, since the town had only a few dozen streets.

"There's a big map in the town square," said the young mother. "I'm sure you'll find it marked there."

The air in the square was tangy with the smells of grilling

meat and spicy falafel. Lamb kebabs sizzled on the flames at an outdoor restaurant. Boys in high-top sneakers and baseball caps hung out under eucalyptus trees. They looked about sixteen—the age Cohen was when I wrote to him.

The map was easy to find, large and well illuminated. Of course, it was in Hebrew. A middle-aged man noticed me studying it in the gathering gloom. I asked if he could help me and showed him the envelope.

"Amme?" he said, baffled. "I don't know such a street." Pinching his fingers together in the universal Middle Eastern gesture that means "Wait a minute," he darted off with my precious letter. I followed, into the Town Hall. A secretary got out the telephone directory and looked up Cohen. My heart sank. Looking for a Cohen in an Israeli phone book struck me as only a little better than trying to look up a Smith in Sydney, or a Kim in Seoul. "There's a Cohen on Amami Street," she said, and proceeded to dial the number.

Of course. Written Hebrew leaves out many vowels. Amme was young Cohen's best try at transliterating the Hebrew word Amami: עממי.

A woman answered. Her voice had the quaver of old age. I asked for Cohen in halting Hebrew.

"*Ma?*" she said. "What? Who wants him?"

I told her Geraldine Brooks, from Australia.

"Jordan Books?" she said, her voice rising with a tinge of alarm. I think she thought I was an Arab publisher. I passed the phone to my helper. His solution to the communication problem was to repeat what I'd said, louder.

"OUR-STRAW-LIAR!" he bellowed.

"Australia," I prompted.

"You're calling all the way from Australia?"

"No! From here, at the Town Hall." The woman, even more confused, muttered something grumpily. "She says the Cohen you want doesn't live there." Disappointment clouded my face. But my translator pinched his fingers together again, in the "Wait a minute" gesture. He listened for a moment, took a pen, scribbled, then put down the phone. "It might be her son. She gave me his number in Netanya." Netanya, a bigger town, lay just a few miles farther north. "But she said he can't know you, because he doesn't speak English."

Could Cohen's mother not realize her son had known enough English to correspond in the language? It seemed unlikely, but the scrawled phone number was the only lead I had. I decided to call it while I still had a Hebrew-speaker on hand. We dialed. No answer. There was nothing to do but thank my helper and head back down the coast to my hotel.

From my room, I tried the number again. This time a younger woman answered, switching quickly from Hebrew to English as she heard my accent. Yes, she said, Cohen lived there. She called him. In Hebrew, I heard her warning him, "She's speaking in English."

Then he was on the line, the disembodied voice of the boy who was the repository of so many teenage fantasies. It was a deep voice, thickly accented with the heavy gutturals of Hebrew-speakers who don't have much practice with English. I tried to explain who I was. His reply, after a long silence, was grave and guarded. Yes, he agreed, he was the Cohen who had lived on Amami Street.

"But I don't remember you," he said.

"Well," I said, "it's a while ago. You were sixteen."

"I was sixteen? But now I'm forty-one!" Silence again. Then, finally, "I don't know what to say." I told him I'd like to meet him. There was yet another long silence. "Why?" he asked. "Why, after so much time?"

It was a question I barely knew how to answer. How could I explain to this taciturn stranger who didn't even remember me that he was part of a fantasy-obsession that shaped my life? I mumbled something about having recently found his letters and wanting to meet him at last. "I'll have to think about it," he said. He took my number and hung up, without even saying goodbye.

I put the phone down, the euphoria of the early evening turned to discouragement. As I tried to sleep, my mind again started spinning scenarios for Cohen, just as I had as a fifteen-year-old. Maybe he was a Mossad agent, and he needed to have me checked out.

I had worried about the logistics of finding my pen pals. It hadn't occurred to me that they might not want to be found.

I was in a heavy jet-lagged sleep when the phone rang at 9 A.M.

"Good morning, how are you?"

It was Cohen, his voice transformed from cold suspicion to friendliness. In the background was the sound of jangly machinery and many people talking. "Can you be at your hotel at 2 P.M. today? Good. I'll come there," he said, and rang off.

Elated, I wandered down to breakfast, my favorite meal in Israel. I loaded the plate with yogurt, cucumber, tomato and smoked fish—an array of foods I'd never dream of eating early in the morning anywhere else—and settled down in a sun-splashed corner of the dining room with a copy of the *Jerusalem Post*. On page 3 there was a story about the effort under way to refill the Hula Swamp. It seemed that the Zionist pioneers had died of malaria and exhaustion in order to perpetrate an environmental atrocity. Now, modern Israel was anxious to redress it.

It was always hard to fathom the pace of change in Israel. The last time I had eaten breakfast in the dining room of that beachside hotel, all the waiters had been Israeli Arabs and the whispered buzz between them as they tidied the buffet and cleared the tables was the gentle murmur of Arabic. Now the staff was entirely Russian, and the muttered words were *"Da, nyet, horosho."* The last time I was there, Arafat had been a hated terrorist in faraway Tunis. Now he was down the highway in Gaza and as much a part of the domestic political landscape as any other outspoken Israeli mayor.

To fill the hours before the meeting with Cohen, I called some correspondent friends in Jerusalem. One of them, an Australian TV reporter, was just back from six weeks home leave in Sydney. She was curious about my pen pals, and I explained that I acquired them because, at the time I was growing up, Sydney felt like the ends of the earth.

"It still feels like the ends of the earth, matie," she said. "For one thing, there's the length of the flight and the feeling that you're getting out at the world's last stop. And then you turn on the TV and there's a whole program about someone who's had a possum piss in their ceiling and can't claim it on insurance. You find yourself thinking, 'If I stay here another six weeks, will I care about that possum, too?'"

I understood why Australia felt remote to her. Living in Israel, she was part of what was perhaps the most plugged-in community on earth. To Israelis, world news was like oxygen. From dangerous neighbors to foreign patrons, there was barely a corner of the planet whose doings were irrelevant.

But, for me, Sydney felt much more globally connected than most American cities. The United States can afford to be insular. It's so big that what happens elsewhere hardly ever matters much. How else to explain the lack of foreign stories on the nightly network news, or the certain social death of being introduced at a cocktail party as someone "just back from Bosnia" or Somalia or, God help you, Eritrea? Suddenly you're trying to converse with someone who appears to be in a stand-up, eyes-open form of deep REM sleep. The mouth gapes soundlessly while the eyeballs dart and spin in search of someone else—anyone else—to talk to.

In Sydney, immigration has been so recent, so diverse, and so extensive that a person you meet at a party may well be from

Bosnia or Eritrea, or their next-door neighbor might be. In the 1991 census, Sydney people listed 271 places of birth outside Australia, or 86 more places than have seats in the United Nations. More than a quarter of the population still speaks a language other than English at home. Israel now is the only country whose population is more culturally diverse, measured by inhabitants' countries of origin.

Cohen called my room promptly at two. I hurried downstairs but couldn't find him by the desk or in the plush lobby. I noticed a man outside on the step, fidgeting. He looked like a taxi driver waiting for a fare. It took awhile until I realized there was no one else who could possibly be Cohen.

He was medium height, thick-set, olive-skinned, with dark curly hair and Ray-Bans. Not Mossad, I decided. Maybe more the shadowy furtive style of a Shin Bet internal security agent. When I greeted him, he seemed edgy. He wouldn't come into the hotel; refused my offer of lunch or a drink. "Let's walk," he said, and so we wandered off down the hotel-lined promenade.

He pointed out his car, a battered blue sedan, parked a few blocks from the hotel. He opened the door and we sat inside, and tried to fill a gap that for me was twenty-four years wide, and that for him, with no memory of having ever written to me, spanned a whole lifetime.

"My mother was very confused when you called her," he said. "I'm confused, too." He remembered nothing of our correspondence, and was stunned when I put his old letters in his hands. "I can't write English so good anymore," he said. He chuckled as he skimmed through the letters with their relentless talk of football. He still played, he said, one night each week.

We picked up his story where the correspondence left off. Cohen had left school and joined the army the year after we stopped writing. He was in an artillery unit when the Yom

Kippur War broke out. During the war's swift and brutal course, he crossed the Sinai. It was all the risk or adventure he ever craved. Forget Mossad and Shin Bet. After the army, he went to work as a teller in a bank, and he had been there ever since.

As the afternoon sun beat on the car, I felt sweat running down my face in tiny rivulets. But gradually, in his halting English, Cohen began to tell me the things he'd never put in his letters.

He was the son of parents who had been part of one of Israel's most dramatic immigrations. They were Yemenite Jews, descendants of the community thought to have arrived in the mountainous toe of the Arabian Peninsula around the time of King Solomon and the Queen of Sheba. Cohen's parents were brought to Israel in the emergency airlift after the 1948 Independence War. In 1949, Yemen was still a medieval society of mudbrick houses ruled by an imam who wanted to protect his people from the corruption of modern life. There were no cars, no hospitals or phones, and the gates of the walled towns closed at sunset.

Yemen's Jews had suffered discrimination. One law said they couldn't ride camels in case a mounted posture raised their heads higher than a Muslim's. But they also had been esteemed for their craftsmanship and learning in a culture that was still largely illiterate. In Israel in 1949, no one needed silversmiths and bookbinders, so the Yemenites became peasants. For years, the people of the airlift were the underclass of Israeli society, more similar in their customs to the Arabs they had lived among for centuries than to Israel's secular European Jews and native-born sabras.

Cohen's father had been only sixteen when he arrived with his bride and was placed in a camp for new immigrants. They were put to work picking oranges. Eventually they scraped together enough money to start their own business and now had a poultry farm with two hundred chickens and a small grocery store.

"It was a very hard life, but you have to understand that my parents believed it was *kodesh*—holy—to come to Israel." Isolated from the rest of the Jewish world for centuries, Yemenite Jews took their faith literally from the pages of the Bible. Before the airlift, they had never seen a plane. But when one arrived to take them, they believed it was a fulfillment of the words of the prophet Isaiah: "They that wait upon the Lord shall renew their strength; they shall mount up with wings as eagles."

As we talked, Cohen became more relaxed and even began to seem pleased that I'd reminded him of a forgotten part of his youth. Before we parted, I asked if he would like to bring his wife to dinner with me at the hotel the following evening. He said he would check with her and give me a call. It was his wife who phoned later that day. In English far more fluent than her husband's she invited me to dinner at their apartment in Netanya.

I expected to be able to locate their place without any difficulty but found myself lost instead in a warren of new streets and apartment-block construction. The huge wave of Russian immigration had flooded once sleepy seaside towns like Netanya. It had become a city in the four years since I had last been there, sprawling north and south in a maze of new streets over sand dunes and uprooted orange groves.

Cohen lived well away from the beach in a vast agglomeration of gray, weather-smeared apartment blocks. Inside, the three-bedroom flat had a hotel-room impersonality. The walls were stark white, free of artworks or knickknacks. The furniture was spare and standard: a leatherette lounge suite, a dark wood-veneer cabinet, a television and a scattering of toys belonging to their four-year-old.

The cool anonymity of it all contrasted with the warmth of Cohen's wife. Ample-hipped, with wide, dark, heavily lashed eyes, she was as outgoing as Cohen was shy, greeting me with a hug and sitting me down at the kitchen table as she served the dinner. Her family also were Yemenites—a huge clan of six brothers and six sisters.

She bustled to and from the refrigerator, chattering as comfortably as if I were an old friend. She had met Cohen through a phone call. "He rang, and I thought he was a friend of my sister's," she said, "so of course I was nice to him, and we chatted for quite a long time. We were laughing and getting on really well when suddenly he realized that he'd dialed the wrong number—he didn't even know my sister."

The two of them decided they'd better meet. "As soon as I saw him I knew he would be my husband."

By this time the kitchen table was covered with an array of dishes: macaroni, mushroom pie, tuna salad, assorted cheeses, Greek salad, avocado, hard-boiled eggs. It was a kosher dairy meal—no meat. But there also was something Arab-style in the way the meal was served: in the mass of items, the wide and plentiful choice, I recognized the kind of meal with which an Arab honors a guest.

In Israel, even ordinary lives brush up against extraordinary situations. The little boy who fidgeted restlessly at the table had been born in the midst of a Scud attack during the war with Iraq in 1991. "I was in labor when the sirens sounded," Cohen's wife recalled. There was no way she could make it to a room sealed against the possibility of poison gas. "I told the nurses just to give me a gas mask and leave me."

She was able to draw on four years of military experience to get her through the ordeal. She had wanted to serve, unlike many Orthodox girls who claim exemption from serving in the army on the grounds that a woman shouldn't take orders from a man not her husband. She loved her job as an army instructor, reenlisting for an additional two years after her first tour expired. Then she went to work for the trade-union movement.

Now she stayed home to look after her son, who was enrolled part time at a religious day-care center. At four years old, he already davened like an ancient rabbi, bobbing and bending as he raced through the Hebrew prayers.

I asked Cohen about his army reserve duty during the intifada. He deflected my query, just as he'd left so many of my questions unanswered when I was his pen pal. But when his wife got up to put their son to bed, he abruptly returned to the subject. He told me quietly that he was sent to quell rioting in the West Bank town of Jenin in December 1987, just as the uprising began. "We had no idea how heavy would be the violence," he said. In those first days the soldiers had no riot gear. Cohen wasn't even wearing a helmet when a teenaged Palestinian dropped a concrete block from a rooftop. "It just missed my head and landed here," he said, leaning forward and touching the vertebrae of his upper back. "I never told my wife."

Technically, Cohen should still have been doing military service for about a month a year until he turned forty-five. But over time the explosions of artillery shells had impaired his hearing and, to his immense relief, the military doctor had recently excused him from serving.

One reason Cohen wasn't needed was that, since the implementation of the 1993 Oslo accords, Israeli soldiers hadn't been required to police the streets of Palestinian villages. "With the Arabs, we give, we give, until maybe we are in the sea. But we have to try. We have no choice."

After dessert—warmed-up packaged blintzes—Cohen pulled out photo albums. Their wedding picture showed a traditional Yemeni bride, decked in a silver cowl and golden veil with a necklace of sweet herbs framing her face and intricate henna patterns painted on her hands. There were pictures of Cohen in the Sinai, a lean teenage warrior, not so different from the fantasy Israeli of my youthful dreams. But that hollow-eyed young man in stained khakis wasn't who Cohen wanted to be. It had been a role imposed on him by a life that I, in my faraway, tranquil Sydney suburb, had romanticized. He, forced to live it, had hated every minute. At the time the photographs were taken he had just seen three of his platoon killed and one have his leg shredded by a mortar. He had no idea how many teenage Egyptian soldiers had been slain in turn by the artillery piece he fired blindly into their positions.

Be careful what you wish for, says the old proverb. You might get it. In peaceful Concord, I had wished for adventures. As a reporter, I'd covered five wars. As Scud missiles threatened the Cohens in Israel, I camped in the Saudi desert with the French Foreign Legion and rafted across the Tigris River with Kurdish guerrillas. In 1991 the Gulf War ended for me in an Easter Sunday trek through mountain passes into Turkey, fleeing Iraq with the thousands of Kurds seeking shelter from Saddam's helicopter gunships.

I arrived home the following weekend, after months away covering the war. I went to see my sister Darleen. After more than twenty years, we were finally living in the same city. But it was London, not Sydney. For foreign correspondents, London was an ideal base from which to cover the Middle East, Africa and the rending of the Iron Curtain. For Darleen, it was the home she'd chosen when she married her English husband Michael. She was working as a magazine editor and raising her two children in an old house on the edge of a woodsy common.

It was a London spring day: wisteria in bud, the dog at my feet shifting his sun-warmed body to scratch a flea. The thought of such days had kept me going during the dull, hot, prewar weeks in Saudi Arabia and the tense, chilly postwar nights in Kurdistan.

My brother-in-law ambled across the terrace with a glass of wine in one hand and the products of his efforts at the barbecue in the other. "Sorry about the sausages," he said. "They're a bit black and crisp."

Black and crisp. Sorry about the rocket, the rubble, the charred flesh, the headless human husk. Black and crisp.

To be a witness to the extremity of human behavior, you have to pay the price of admission.

> *What is the price of experience?* asks William Blake.
> *Do men buy it for a song?*
> *Or wisdom for a dance in the street? No.*
> *It is bought with the price*
> *Of all that a man hath, his house, his wife, his children.*

Journalists usually get their experience at a discount. When we go to war we rarely die, we don't have to kill, our homes aren't pounded to rubble, we aren't cast adrift as exiles. If we are bruised at all, it is by the images we carry, the memories we wish we didn't have. I would always have them, dark pictures in a mental album that I could never throw away.

I had been so cavalier, as a teenager in Sydney, about willing experiences on other people. As we gazed at the pictures in Cohen's photo album, I could only imagine what the contents of his mental album must be like. As a reporter, I had only visited the front lines of wars. I hadn't had to stay there, battle after battle, breathing the stink of dried blood and rotting flesh. By the time the adrenalin rush wore off, I was back somewhere safe, generally somewhere with room service.

I had wanted Cohen to be a brave Zionist warrior, when all he'd coveted was a quiet suburban life just like the one in Sydney that I was so busily wishing away. Even after the determined ordinariness of his letters, I'd continued to wish drama upon him. A day or two earlier, I'd been ready to sign him up as a shadowy secret policeman or a remorseless spy. I studied the real Cohen—the shy banker slumped contentedly beside me on the sofa—and set him free at last from the heavy burden of my imaginings.

There wasn't much more to say to each other. As I rose to leave, I mentioned I was heading on to Nazareth, to try to find my other long-ago pen pal. Cohen wrinkled his brow. Although Nazareth lies only a couple of hours' drive from Netanya, Cohen had never ventured there. When he said so, my eyebrows rose in surprise. Israel is tiny—the size of New Jersey, one fortieth the size of my Australian home state of New South Wales. I couldn't imagine living a lifetime in such a small place and not exploring every inch of it.

But Cohen merely shrugged. "Why would I go? I don't know anyone in Nazareth," he said. "Aren't you afraid to go there, a woman alone?"

Why should I be afraid? Nazareth, after all, wasn't the West Bank. It was part of Israel. Its Arab citizens had been Israelis since 1948—a year longer than Cohen's own Yemenite parents.

Yes, he nodded, that was so. "But still, they are Arabs."

Still, they are Arabs, and when I turned my car westward at Haifa and headed into the Galilee, I felt I had crossed an invisible border. In that region of Israeli-Arab towns and villages, the roads suddenly got rougher, and soon I heard a dull thunk as my right front wheel dropped into a gaping pothole.

In the proclamation of Israeli independence in May 1948, the Jewish leaders called upon the Arab inhabitants of the state of Israel to "play their part in the development of the State on the basis of full and equal citizenship." I knew that proclamation by heart; it was part of the arsenal I had unleashed so long ago on my Palestinian schoolmate Monique, in our history class arguments.

While Monique didn't have her facts tidily marshaled in

those days, she had been right when she replied that Arabs who stayed had never enjoyed full and equal citizenship. Instead, they were placed under military rule until 1966—required to get a pass from the army to travel from one part of their own country to another.

Even now, the contrast in government spending between Arab and Jewish areas remained stark. And that contrast had just cost me a front tire. My lame car limped to the side of the road and I got out to inspect the damage. I barely had the trunk open to search for the spare when the very first car to pass by pulled over. The young Arab driver was the first of three who stopped to offer aid. It was an instant reminder of the reflexive hospitality Arabs show to strangers. If one had to have a flat tire, this probably was one of the best stretches of road in the world on which to have it.

On the way into Nazareth the road narrowed and wound as the hills rose abruptly, covered in a honeycomb of tightly packed houses. Everything about Nazareth was unmistakably Arab: the style of the buildings, their dense asymmetry, the arabesque winding of the narrow streets. The city's status as a Christian pilgrimage site was evident from the churches, convents and abbeys in almost every block. In the 1920s the Arabs of the town were ninety percent Christian. Since then, Muslim Arabs had moved in from the villages, and many Christians had emigrated. Nuns' habits shared the streets with Muslim veils, and the occasional minaret of a mosque popped up like an exotic plant in the forest of church spires and crucifixes.

I found the pilgrims' hotel where I had booked a room. It had been impossible to get much information about Nazareth hotels from the Israeli tourist desk at Ben Gurion Airport. The young clerk had offered me a detailed, rated list of inns and B&Bs in the nearby Jewish suburb, Nazret Illit. But for establishments in the old Arab town itself there were just names and phone numbers, no ratings. I soon discovered that in the hotel I'd chosen the emphasis on the word "pilgrim" was clearly on the "grim." My bed was hard and monastically narrow, the shower cold.

In the morning I woke to the unmistakably Arabian aroma of cardamom-scented coffee. Fortified by a strong, sticky cupful, I set out with my map. I figured that Nazareth's numbered street plan should make it easy to find the address.

But if Nazareth once had an orderly grid system, years of weaving in extra alleys and laneways has turned it into a spaghetti tangle of streets where numbers seem to have been assigned at random. By late morning, as the sun crept higher, I had trudged in circles and ventured down blind alleys until I'd become a dusty, sweaty mess.

Defeated, I backtracked to the tourist office and threw myself on a chair beneath the air conditioner. The smiling woman behind the desk showed no interest in the address. "Maybe I know the family?" she said. "Then I can tell you where they live." Nazareth, with a population of more than 70,000, operated like a small town. Although the young woman didn't recognize the family name, she directed me to a taxi company whose drivers, she said, "know everybody."

At the taxi kiosk the manager got on the radio and out of a blur of static managed to find a driver who knew my pen pal's family. Soon we were outside the gate of a tall building more like an apartment block than a house. Beyond a jasmine-draped courtyard an external staircase ran up the side of a layer-cake structure, each level looking slightly newer than the one beneath.

When I rang the bell a dapper, elderly man emerged from the ground floor, smiling broadly as if I was the exact person he most hoped to see. I barely had the words "Australia" and "Mishal" out of my mouth when he had an arm around me, propelling me inside, insisting on paying the twenty shekels I owed the cab driver, who then refused to accept the fare because he was a friend of a friend of the family.

"Come in, come in, meet my wife," said my ebullient host, almost dancing on the balls of his feet. "I'm Mishal's father, of course. We remember you—he wrote to you all those years ago. We can't allow you to stay in a hotel. You must sleep here in our house—you are like my daughter while you are here in Nazareth. My daughter lives here of course. All my children do. You can't buy land in Nazareth; it's very expensive, so we stay all together here and the house grows up with the children. Mishal is the oldest—but you know that already. Four married, three grandchildren and one more on the way. So you will stay here with all of us. We have a saying in Arabic: mountains can't meet each other but people can."

Mishal's father hadn't paused for breath. "I'm just back from traveling myself, in Germany, and I had some wonderful hospitality there. Somebody stole my bag at the airport and the Jewish community gave me two hundred deutschmarks. I could speak to them in Yiddish, because I learned it growing up in Haifa. You don't speak German, I suppose? Or French? My German and French are better than my English."

It was hard to imagine how his other languages could be any more fluent than the rapid-fire monologue he'd just delivered.

"But what are we thinking? We must call Mishal and tell him that his old friend is here. And we must give you something to eat, drink. You must be hungry."

His wife, smiling, gently told him that she had already called Mishal, who was on his way home. She also already had set down a Coke and a plate of fruit in front of me. Fragrant coffee bubbled on the stove in a bright kitchen where the bench space overflowed with fresh-picked olives, ripening tomatoes and glossy eggplants.

The sitting room—full of heavy furniture that Mishal's father had French-polished to a deep sheen—was dark. Mishal's mother suggested we pull our chairs out to the small vine-covered courtyard. The scent of jasmine made me homesick for Sydney.

"Mishal has no children, after twelve years of marriage," his mother confided abruptly. In Arabic, the standard, mannerly reply to this news is *"Allah kareem."* The words literally translate as "God is generous," but in this society of tight-knit extended families, the meaning is entirely the opposite. I suppose his mother felt it necessary to blurt out the information so that I wouldn't embarrass Mishal by asking.

A few minutes later a tall man bounded up the steps. At forty-one, his hair was silvery. Like Cohen, he had a slight paunch. He was covered in a fine mist of sawdust. Mishal was a carpenter.

He grabbed my hand and pumped it. "It's great to see you," he said, as if it were only a week or two since we'd written to each other. Like me, Mishal had lots of pen pals. There was a boy in Malaysia, a girl in Germany. And his interest in the wide world seemed to have been inspired by his father, just as mine had.

Reaching for a panama hat from the hall stand, Mishal's father excused himself with a slight bow. "I hope you will forgive me: I have to get the newspapers before they are all sold," he said. "One has to know what is happening in this world, after all." He straightened his silk tie and made his way, slowly but somehow jauntily, up the steep hill to the main street.

Mishal smiled. "Every day, he has to read every newspaper, he has to watch all the news programs. Now that we've got satellite, he can watch CNN and all the German news as well. Me, I don't like politics. I like to work, make money, go places."

Mishal's thirty-two-year-old wife worked too, packing sweets for grocery stores in her brother's small warehouse in the village of Cana, the site of Jesus' first miracle. Mishal asked if I'd like to go and see the church there before he picked her up from work. On the way he had to call on some clients, and asked if I'd mind tagging along.

As a reporter in Arab countries, I'd often found myself swept up like this, welcomed midstream into the routines of someone's daily life. We drove through the warren of old Arab Nazareth and up toward the new Jewish suburb, Nazret Illit, that sat on the ridgetop like a sentinel. As we entered the newer town the maze of cracked sidewalks and twisting alleyways was replaced by a tidy geometry of new apartments and wide, curbed streets. I wondered if Mishal resented this place, which after all was built on land that the overcrowded Arab city might have used for its own expansion.

But in Israel's confusing way, nothing was quite what it seemed. For Mishal, Nazret Illit was a rich source of clients. We climbed the stairs to a brand new apartment where Mishal was finishing off a kitchen for a family of Russian immigrants. The apartment's owner greeted him warmly. She was Christian, like Mishal. As Mishal measured counter tops, she explained that though her husband was born Jewish he had lived all his life in Russia as a Christian to avoid discrimination. It took only one Jewish grandparent to be eligible to migrate to Israel, and many Russian families made the move because prospects in the former Soviet Union looked grim for Jews and non-Jews alike. In many cases the Jewish grandparent was the one member of the family who elected to stay behind, while the Christian members took advantage of the only chance they would ever have to move to a country that welcomed them.

"Many of these people are my clients now," Mishal said. Such families often had more in common with fellow Christians, even if Arab, than they did with the Jews.

As we headed out of Nazret Illit the road narrowed again and wound through fields of wild fennel and olive groves. In the distance lumpy Mount Tabor rose from the plain, a sudden geological thumbs-up sign. As we drove into Cana, the road to the old church was crowded with pilgrims. There were groups from Brazil, clusters of African-Americans, a Japanese couple and a band of Italians. We picked up Mishal's wife, a petite, soft-spoken woman with a generous smile, and headed home.

When we returned, Mishal's father was glued to the news on CNN. "Arnett!" he cried as the correspondent's face filled the screen, reporting from Bosnia, where NATO jets had just bombed a Serb hospital. "America *shamouta*!" he cried. *Shamouta* is Arabic for whore. "In Sudan, Turabi is killing Christians for years," he said, referring to the endless war against the Sudanese Christians who refused to live under Muslim laws. "Why doesn't America do something for *them*?" Watching him argue so passionately with the TV reminded me of my own father, and how much I missed all the irascible energy his illness had drained away.

Mishal and his wife signaled me to follow them up the outside staircase to their own apartment. Their flat was about the same size as Cohen's but opposite in atmosphere. Almost every square inch of wall was covered with landscape prints, huge glossy photographs of gladiolus or pale oak shelves built by Mishal to support an array of knickknacks: artificial flower arrangements, pharaonic souvenirs from a holiday in Egypt, a Greek Orthodox silver-framed icon of the Virgin, a miniature water pipe and a sea of snapshots of nieces and nephews.

After dinner of hummus, olives, salad, and eggplant stuffed with peppery beef, we rejoined the family on the terrace, munching roasted pumpkin seeds in the warm evening air. Mishal's father had moved on from barking at CNN to berating the Arabic newspaper. On the front page was an account of the murder of a Jewish man and the stabbing of his pregnant wife in a West Bank settlement. The newspaper used the word *shaheed,* or martyr, to describe the murderer. "They think they go straight to heaven, these so-called *shaheed*. They think they get paradise—beautiful ladies, a stream of water and a nice view. Ha! When you're dead *halas*—it's finished. No ladies. No view."

That night I slept in Mishal's spare room—what might have been the child's room. As if to underscore that absence, a huge blue plush bear sat in one corner, still wrapped in plastic. I fell asleep to the familiar street sounds of Arab cities: the gentle murmurs of the late night promenaders, the raucous honking of overused car horns, the lonely crow of an insomniac rooster pealing from a neighbor's rooftop coop.

I woke with a start to a loud voice singing. It took me a moment to recognize the Muslim call to prayer. For almost six years, when I was a Middle East correspondent, that call had been as familiar to me as the beep of an alarm clock. Lying there, I reflected on how my years writing to Mishal—the surprise of finding more of a kindred spirit in him than in Cohen—had made it easier for me to take the Middle East job when it was offered. His letters had humanized the Arab world and taught me to look beneath the stereotypes and the scary headlines. He was the prototype for the many Arabs who had become my friends.

Outside, as the sun eased up, the honeycomb of buildings on the far hill turned from rose to gold to pearly white. A ray of sunshine glanced off the glass of a framed document on the bedroom wall—Mishal's high school diploma. I studied his grades: they were excellent. I wondered why he hadn't gone on to university.

At breakfast I steered the conversation around to a point where I could politely ask. Mishal's reply was matter-of-fact. To go to university, he felt, would have pushed him up against a glass ceiling confronting Israeli Arabs. As an independent tradesman, he could make a good living. But if he had become, say, an engineer, he would have had to find work either with the Israeli government or with private firms that preferred Jews. Israeli Arabs are exempt from military service, which is a mixed blessing in a country where a good army record is a basic job credential.

Mishal explained all this with no apparent resentment. I probed for some, but nothing surfaced. I hadn't mentioned my own conversion, so there was no reason for him to tailor his opinions to my sensibilities. "Jews are good people," he said. "They want to live and this is the only place they've got." He said he'd never experienced discrimination. "I've heard people say that in Tel Aviv someone's yelled, 'Dirty Arab'—but it's never happened to me. This is the best place for an Arab, really. I don't bother the Jews, they don't bother me. The standard of living is high, and you are free to say whatever you like."

"We get the brains from all over the world here," his father added. "German doctors, Russian scientists. I don't care if they're Jews or not Jews. It's Babel—we're all speaking a different language but we're building something together."

I wished my dad was with me to hear all this. Mishal and his father inhabited the idealized Israel that Lawrie believed in, the place I'd come to think of as a propaganda myth. For years I had thought that the pro-Israeli views in Mishal's letters to me were his tactful reaction to my own ardent, adolescent Zionism. But after spending time with him and his family it was clear to me that the views were, after all, his real beliefs.

It was Saturday, and Mishal wanted to use his day off taking me on a tour of his favorite sights. We drove to the Jordan River and circled the Sea of Galilee. As we gazed at the ancient monuments and the fertile farms, he was as proud of them as any Jewish Israeli. Even the new settlements earned praise from him, although more land under Jewish construction left less room for Arab towns to expand. Mishal had worked for the affluent professionals in one deluxe cluster of new villas, and with a word to the security guard we were waved inside the gated community. "No one is looking at what his neighbor is doing here," Mishal said wistfully. "He has a drink, he sees a woman friend—they mind their own business." He didn't say it, but the contrast to his own unprivate life in the family compound and in Nazareth's overgrown-village atmosphere was obvious.

He showed me the kibbutz where he worked for over a year as carpenter in residence, repairing locks, squaring wobbly tables, making doors close snugly. He enjoyed the communal meals in the dining hall. "Breakfast was nice," he said, "good yogurt, fresh avocado and fruit, cheese and eggs." He liked the way nobody fussed about the kibbutz girls in their thigh-high shorts. "Nobody's looking at her—it's a normal thing," he said. By contrast, an Arab friend had refused to go with him to a hot-springs spa because they didn't have separate hours for men and women, and the friend worried about people looking at his wife. "She's not young, she's had kids, nobody's interested," said Mishal. "But that's the mentality."

On the way back we picked up some food for dinner. Mishal liked to buy fresh milk and fruit from a particular Jewish *moshav*. Farther on, he turned up a winding dirt road where an old Bedouin in a Brooks Brothers shirt and crisply pressed pants lived amid scratching hens and rusty farm machinery. The old man poured us coffee from a long-spouted brass pot set on a brazier, and haggled with Mishal over the price of his wife's fresh-made cheese.

"If my father was with us, he'd insist we go to Jenin for some bargain-price vegetables," said Mishal, but he didn't think the saving was worth the detour to the West Bank town.

Still, it was clear that Mishal moved easily between the three worlds of Jews, Israeli Arabs and West Bank Palestinians. I thought of Cohen: anxious about Nazareth, an enemy in Jenin. Mishal's Israel was a much bigger place.

Driving away from Nazareth later that night, I felt relaxed in a way I rarely had before on journeys to Israel. As a reporter there, my business had most often been the seeking of extremes. Reporters look for the quotable people, the articulate. Unsurprisingly, those people turn out to be the hotheads, the passionately committed. Meanwhile, real life is happening elsewhere, in the middle, among the Mishals and the Cohens, who care more about their families and jobs than ideology. These people are elusive to journalists precisely because they aren't out wielding a placard or writing an op-ed or even all that ready with a fully formed opinion if stopped on a street corner.

But it may be in the quiet center, among the bankers of Netanya and the carpenters of Nazareth, that the real history of a place is written after all. As another carpenter from Nazareth observed a long time ago, it is the meek who shall inherit the earth.

11

Cherchez
la Femme

⚜

The rented Renault made an ugly sound as it struggled up the mountain incline. Outside, little pinhead snowflakes fell gently from a steel-gray December sky. In the highlands set back from the coast, the famed mild winters of the South of France can be raw and bone-chilling.

I raised my voice over the engine's wheeze. " 'Motte d' Aigue,' " I read to Tony. "We're looking for a village called 'Lump of Points.' "

Theoretically, St. Martin de la Brasque would lie just beyond. But it was hard to be sure. The village didn't make it onto any of the local maps. And no one seemed to have heard of the place.

On either side of us the mountains of the Lubéron rose green in their year-round sheath of oaks and cedars, pines and stunted thymes. Rows of vines, hard-pruned for winter, quilted the valley floor. Their leaves had turned red, then yellow, and fallen. And the saws had been through, turning summer's generous sprawls into two-armed skeletons shaking nubby fists at the louring sky.

It was Cézanne's landscape, and I loved it, as I continued to love so much that was French: the poetry, the novels, the films, the cuisine, and the beautiful little corner of the Alpes Maritimes where Darleen and Michael had built a whitewashed house on a couple of terraced acres. On a brilliantly sunny December day in 1984, Tony and I had been married there.

But there was so much about France that I had also come to despise: the murderous arrogance of French nuclear testing in the Pacific, the corrupt self-interest of French foreign policy in the Middle East.

I was living in Sydney in 1986 when a French government bomb blew up the Greenpeace protest boat, *Rainbow Warrior,* in a New Zealand harbor, killing a young Portuguese photographer. At the time I was working for an Australian weekly, the *National Times,* and I wrote a cover story on the bombers that was illustrated by the Tricolor of France, scrawled with the French word for shit, *merde.*

The day the issue appeared, I got a call from the local *Le Monde* reporter, who thought her readers would find this flag desecration arresting. She wanted a comment on what it revealed about Australian attitudes toward France. I told her that most Australians saw the French as scumbag international outlaws, and then I invited her over to my place for a garlic-studded gigot wrapped in fresh rosemary.

Sylvie turned out to be much more the sort of correspondent I'd had in mind when I wrote away for a French pen pal in 1968. She came to dinner with her partner, Jean-Pierre, who had actually been a cobblestone hurler of that angry Paris spring, one of the *beaux étudiants avec colère* I'd admired on the TV news.

Jean-Pierre had tossed his engineering studies to become a Maoist intellectual, one of the founders of the leftist newspaper

Libération. But by the time I met him in the mid-1980s, France's conservatives were once again in the ascendant. Jean-Pierre's tousled curls had started to turn silver and his little boy was about to turn two. He sat at my table, swirling the wine in his glass as the gigot turned slowly over the open fire. "Paris," he said. The boredom in his voice turned the word into a sigh, followed by a sound that defied accurate transliteration—part raspberry, part jeer. "It is finished for me."

He yearned, he said, to encounter "something primitive." He proposed to explore the Outback. I saw them off from Sydney—their toddler Benjamin clutching the last baguette he would see in months. I hoped that what they found wouldn't be more primitive than he bargained for.

In central Australia they were bewitched by Aboriginal art—the richly colored Dreamtime maps through which individuals passed on pieces of the store of tribal knowledge. The paintings spoke the language of the desert landscape with a fluency few other works had matched. At a time when only a handful of Australians appreciated these paintings, Jean-Pierre and Sylvie became connoisseurs. Soon they were mounting major exhibitions back in France.

When an invitation arrived for the first big show in Montpellier, I smiled. I thought about the day my sister had taken me to see the Rodin sculptures. I wondered if there would be a little girl in Montpellier whose love affair with art would begin as she stared at those powerful, mysterious images of a faraway desert and a life at the ends of the earth.

In December 1995, France exploded in the worst unrest the country had seen since those heady days in 1968. Everywhere, workers were striking and rioting in protest at government attempts to dismantle social security and favorable work rules.

Tony and I read accounts of the unrest with growing interest. During our years as Foreign Correspondents, arriving in places just as other people rushed to get out of them, we'd learned that troubled times often made for great tourism opportunities: empty hotels, uncrowded sightseeing, bargain prices. It was close to our wedding anniversary. We could have a romantic visit to the site of our nuptials, catch up with Sylvie and Jean-Pierre in Montpellier, and do what I'd longed to do since finding Janine's old letters: search for the elusive village of St. Martin de la Brasque in the foothills of the Lubéron.

EN GRÈVE read the hand-lettered sign at Marseilles airport, where a strike by customs officers left no one to check bags. *EN GRÈVE* read a similar sign on the unmanned tollbooths of the autoroute, where no one waited to collect the usual fistful of francs. And, just as we'd anticipated, since everyone was *en grève,* no one was *en vacances.*

Our hotel, a converted olive mill in the village of Lourmarin, was empty. As a result, the manageress upgraded the modest room we'd reserved to the best suite, on the top floor, with a balcony overlooking the château and the fields beyond.

In the morning she had plenty of time to talk to us about the charms of the region as we sipped our café au lait. But her rich vein of local knowledge ended abruptly when we asked her about St. Martin de la Brasque. Placing another log on the fire, she paused, raised an eyebrow and curled her lip, converting her face into a bouquet of rococo squiggles. *"Phut,"* she said. If the British have a stiff upper lip, the French definitely have at least one extra facial muscle to facilitate these magnificent sneers. "I know nothing about it. *Rien.*"

The only map in our possession that gave us any hint of St. Martin's location was the one on a tourist postcard that Janine had sent me years ago showing the Vaucluse region. Vaucluse means "the closed valley." Janine lived somewhere between the Grand Lubéron mountains and the Durance River. On the postcard she had underlined the town of Pertuis, and on the back she had written that St. Martin was *"près de cette ville."*

As we finished our coffee, the manageress made some phone calls. She returned with the news that St. Martin was in fact only five villages east of Lourmarin. "But it is nothing," she reported. "It's a town of truck drivers, vineyard workers and people who work in eggs."

"Eggs? They have poultry farms?"

"No—Eggs—it's the big town south of here."

Aix. Aix-en-Provence. St. Martin was a village of laborers and commuters.

As Tony and I drove up the mountainside past the patchwork of vineyards, I imagined Janine's father working his meticulous way through the vines, knowing from experience where to prune, where to let be. It was he I thought we would find in St. Martin, if we ever found St. Martin. I hoped he would be able to tell me news of his daughter, my bright young pen pal from so many years ago. Janine herself, I imagined, would be long gone from these little villages; pursuing a career in nearby Marseilles, Montpellier, Lyon or maybe even Paris.

Finally St. Martin announced itself with a modest sign and an avenue of speckled plane trees. In a minute or two it disannounced itself with a duplicate sign, slashed through by a black bar. Now I understood why, when I wrote to Janine, I didn't need to give a street address—her name and the name of the village were all the direction my letters required.

We turned the car around and drove back through the village, more slowly. Many of the old sepia-stuccoed houses had gray, concrete block additions. Some had been torn down and replaced with boxy new structures. Apart from the handsome row of trees, St. Martin felt no obligation to be picturesque. We parked in the square. It was still lunchtime, and the town's few streets were silent. The faint snow had turned to a misty, Londonesque drizzle. A lone old man and his black and white dog ambled slowly down the street.

We left the car and wandered to the bar-tabac, into that familiar warm French fug of fresh-ground coffee and strong tobacco. The walls were decorated with the important business of village life: the standings of the Martinoise boule players and the latest news from the Société des Chasseurs. Inside, the sole customer stood hunched over a pinball machine called Star Flipp, emblazoned with an icon of Marilyn Monroe. Like the rest of France, the machine appeared to be *en grève*. The youth thumped it petulantly, but no bells rang.

We ordered a coffee and asked the barmaid if she knew the family of my pen pal. *"Oui,"* she said. *"Bien sûr."*

"You know *Janine?"* I asked.

"Mais oui, elle habit . . ." and she rattled off directions to a house on the town's edge.

Even after my experiences in Israel, I almost fell off my bar stool in shock. After twenty-five years, Janine was still there, right where I left her. The barmaid said Janine had married a builder and managed his business from her house. "If you want to find her at home, now would be a good time," she said. "Soon she will have to go to pick up her boys from school."

We drained our bitter coffees and headed for the eastern edge of town. In a few minutes, following the barmaid's directions, we had arrived at the foot of a steep hill dotted with newish, modest-scale villas. On the unfinished balcony of one of them a builder was at work. But by the time I got out of the car and climbed up to the house he had vanished. I walked on to the next villa and knocked on the door.

A young man answered.

"Excuse me," I said in French, "I'm looking for Janine."

"Oui," he said. He turned back into the house and raised his voice to call the name. A petite woman in a big sweater and

leggings appeared at the door. Her dark hair was cropped in a shapely bob that emphasized her soft brown eyes.

As I introduced myself, I opened my hand and showed her one of the letters she'd sent me, the elegant writing on the pretty pale blue stationery. She stared at me and then at the letters. Her hand fluttered to her brow.

"But it is twenty years—no—more," she said in French.

Still, she remembered me well. I had been her only pen friend. She explained that I had knocked, by chance, on her mother's door. Her house was nearby, but she was spending the day with her mother, who was ill. She seemed anxious to talk, so we made a rendezvous for the following day.

Janine's parents' house in the village had long since been demolished, its cramped, medieval rooms too small and irregular for modern taste. Her entire family lived now in new villas on the hillside, all built by Janine's husband.

Janine's villa was the last on the curve of terrace, before the pines and scrub oak reclaimed the mountainside. Patches of raw concrete, a cement mixer parked by the entrance and churned-up mud in the driveway gave the house that unfinished look so common to the homes of architects and builders too busy working on others' projects to get the last touches done on their own. But tucked away on adjoining terraces were a big swimming pool, drained for winter, and a separate clubhouse-cum-games room complete with pizza oven and pinball machine.

Janine greeted me at the door and ushered me into a large room that overlooked the valley below. From this terraced hillside the valley stretched away in a long misty view of vineyards and orchards. From here, it was easy to understand why someone born in this place might never leave it.

A fire blazed in the hearth, its fuel the wood from those same vineyards. At first I mistook the wood for prunings, but then I noticed that the pieces of vine stacked to dry by the hearth had roots attached.

"They are pulling up many vineyards these days," Janine explained. "It is my father's work now." The Lubéron had never been one of France's great wine regions. What it supplied was vin ordinaire, and these days other wine regions—including Australia's—were filling that market more cheaply. The vintners no longer had a market for so many grapes, so Janine's father was spending the last few years of his working life grubbing up the vineyards he had spent years nurturing into productivity. "Then he sells them for firewood," Janine explained.

I realized that I had seen her father on the terrace by her mother's house. A big, bereted man with a weathered face, he was maneuvering a tractor loaded high with vines. I had thought the scene picturesque. Now it seemed melancholy.

The table decoration spoke to another link with the land. Instead of a vase of flowers, a large dish of sprouting wheat grains occupied the center of the table. "Is it your son's science project?" I asked. Janine laughed. "No. It is a tradition for the time of year. You start the grains at the beginning of December, and if they are high and green by Christmas it means you will have a rich harvest in the coming year."

Since our brief meeting the day before, Janine had found a photo I had sent her of myself. She had placed it on the mantel. It was the picture I had sent in 1969—the one that I'd thought made me look angry and radical. What I really looked like was a kid who'd forgotten to brush her hair.

I'd hoped Janine would speak English as well as she wrote it as a sixteen-year-old. But she had forgotten everything. As she glanced at her own letters, she said she now couldn't decipher the English sections she had written so flawlessly.

My French had improved a bit since I left school, because I had been forced to use it while reporting in North Africa and when visiting my sister in the nearby Alpes Maritimes. I also had assistance from Tony, who didn't share my tin ear for pronunciation. But Janine's accent gave us both some trouble. It was heavily Provençal, with words like *bien* becoming "bang" and *main* becoming "meng." The conversation proceeded in a choppy relay, with Janine often repeating herself, me kibbitzing with Tony on what she'd said, the two of us figuring out a response and Tony saying it in an accent she could comprehend.

Janine hadn't had any reason to use English since she left school. The ruthless selectivity of the French educational system had directed her to a secretarial course. She was twenty when she met and married Juan, a Spanish immigrant whose family had come to the nearby town of Pertuis when he was nine.

"We came because we wanted to eat," said Juan, who had wandered in with a large hunting rifle slung over his shoulder. He was a tall, handsome man with curly blond hair and a tanned face etched deeply by laughter lines. There had been no work in his parents' home town of Valencia. "There was a lot of racism when we came, but now we are French," he said with a convincingly Gallic shrug. These days, it was the more recently arrived Algerian and Moroccan immigrants who bore the stigma of foreignness.

This corner of provincial, rural, France had been all Juan and Janine had ever needed. At the age of forty, Janine had never visited Paris. I'd longed to see Paris, even though I'd had to travel halfway around the world to do it. For Janine, it was a day's drive that she'd never bothered to take.

There was a wedding picture of Juan and Janine hanging on the wall. "Actually, it is a picture of one of our weddings," Janine explained. France's Napoleonic laws are even stricter in their separation of church and state than those of the United States. Religious wedding ceremonies aren't legally recognized and have to be preceded by a civil marriage. In 1984, Tony and I had two French weddings, the first presided over by a mayor whose tricolor sash sat majestically across his impressive embonpoint. The next day a rabbi married us again, under a chuppa rigged from Tony's grandmother's shawl and some pieces of wood bought at the last minute from the local *bricolage*.

Janine's situation was even more complicated. Her family was Protestant, a remnant of the Vaudois—a medieval movement considered heretical by the Catholic Church. In the sixteenth century brutal religious wars between Catholics and Protestants decimated Lubéron towns, including St. Martin. Juan was Roman Catholic. So they had to be married at the mayor's in St. Martin, then at the Protestant church in Lourmarin, then at the Catholic church in Pertuis. Since then, they had raised three boys—now seventeen, fourteen and nine—"all of them," laughed Janine, "with no religion!"

Juan had taken his rifle out of its canvas covering, disassembled it and was cleaning the parts carefully on the dining-room table. When I asked what he had been hunting, he pulled from a sack a brace of small blood-speckled birds. Using one tiny corpse like a hand puppet, he made the bird's beak open and close as he trilled an imitation of its call.

"Will you cook them?" I asked Janine, thinking they would provide poor fare for three hungry boys. Janine shuddered. "No, I have nothing to do with this . . . this . . . hobby . . . of his. I hate killing. Juan loves to hunt, but I make him give away what he kills." In return, sometimes, people brought her samples of what they made from her husband's trophies. She went to the kitchen and returned with some home-canned pâté, made by a neighbor after Juan had a good day in pursuit of grebes. It was, I had to acknowledge, averting my eyes from the corpses of their relatives, delicious.

From September through January, Juan scheduled his building projects to allow maximum time for *la chasse* through the piny woods of the Lubéron. When he was home, he cleaned guns, listened to an electronic bird-call imitator that helped him identify quarry or tended his hunting dogs. He asked if I wanted to see his kennels.

We scrambled together up the steep slope behind the house. Behind a high wire fence, more than a dozen tails wagged. The dogs were kept four to a pen, and inside each pen was a doggy-sized villa, complete with stucco walls and traditional Provençal red roof tiles. Juan went from pen to pen, speaking to each dog and doling out dinner—a mixture of kibble, yesterday's baguettes and tasty-looking leftover *daube*. As he introduced each dog he explained its strong points like a proud father. Some were retrievers, skilled at finding the tiny corpses of blasted songbirds. Others had the courage for running down the big-tusked, drooling *sanglier*, or wild boar.

When we returned to the house I asked Janine how she liked the dogs. "I have asthma, so I don't like them too well," she replied dryly. I had often wondered how couples cope when one has a passionate interest that the other finds dull or distasteful. But I had rarely seen such an extreme case as this one.

It was almost time for Janine to pick up her youngest son. Together, we drove back into the town square to wait for the school bus from nearby Pertuis.

Janine greeted the other mothers in the square. She had grown up with all of them, their lives lived together in the lockstep of a small village. Thirty years earlier, they'd taken the bus together as children. Now they waited for it together, as mothers. While they waited, they chatted, as they had the day before, and almost every other day of their lives. It was the kind of continuity that never existed in a restless new country like Australia, where people are always moving in and moving on. I thought of our street in Concord: none of the neighbors of my parents' generation had been born there, and none of my generation had stayed.

When the school bus arrived Janine's son emerged looking

tired from his long school day and almost staggering under a bookbag-rucksack packed heavily enough for a five-day wilderness trek.

Janine chatted with him about his homework on the short drive home. At the dining-room table she sat down with him, spread out his textbooks and went over that night's requirements for every subject. As she returned to me in the sitting room, he went uncomplainingly to work on what looked set to be several hours of study.

As the light drained from the sky, we said our goodbyes. Tony and I climbed into the car and headed back down the hills toward Lourmarin.

All those years ago, I had written to Janine because I was hungry for the wide world, and yet my letters had found their way to this narrow sliver of provincial village life. In the years since we wrote to each other, as my world had expanded, hers had contracted. Janine and her husband, and the extended family surrounding them, lived a life that was as unchanged in its essence as the little village of St. Martin itself. Juan's rifles may have been made of modern alloys, but men here had always hunted. His construction company may have used cranes and reinforced concrete, but the craft of building a house wasn't that different from the one pursued here by sixteenth-century masons. And Janine's world, caring for her children and her aged parents, living a life in a place where she knew not just every person but every stone, could be the same intimate world of a woman born in many centuries other than the present one.

The next night we found ourselves in the France of my teenage fantasy, aloft on a thermal of intellectual hot air. The walls of the art gallery were white and floodlit, providing a good background both for the avant-garde art and the even more avant patrons. The men wore long black trench coats, the women short black skirts. The conversation bounced from aesthetics to the strike and to politics in general. It was my stereotypical French scene, animated to order from a dusty corner of my youthful imagination.

Tony stood in contemplation of one work—a pink velour soft-toy mouse with its stuffing removed, nailed to a well-worn kitchen cutting board.

"It represents Mickey—an international icon of good and evil," explained the artist, a tall, gaunt, stringy-haired man clad in leather. "As Baudelaire says, we must examine the morality of the toy."

Tony raised a questioning eyebrow.

"The mouse Mickey, he is supposedly benign, cheerful, and yet he is also the leering face of global cultural imperialism."

"Oh," said Tony. "And what about the cutting board?"

"The icon, the mouse Mickey, he is crucified on a surface that is ambiguous also," said the artist. "The cutting board is an object used to create sustenance, but also to dissect flesh."

We moved on to the next room, where a second artist had taped his unframed work to the walls. They were small pages of text with a few calligraphic arrows and an occasional doodlish line drawing.

"It's a synthesis of alchemy and tantra," explained the second artist, an older, plumper man also clad in leather. "It's post-postmodern."

Our friends Jean-Pierre and Sylvie noticed the glazed look in our eyes and decided it was time for dinner. Saying farewell to their artist friends, they shepherded us toward a cozy restaurant.

Jean-Pierre and Sylvie were back in France in between trips to arrange exhibitions of Tibetan tiger rugs and Navajo sand paintings. Their work with the paintings of the Aborigines had grown into a worldwide campaign to draw attention to art of threatened cultures everywhere.

Inside the restaurant, Jean-Pierre took off his jacket to reveal a faded green T-shirt emblazoned with the word "Australia." I assumed he'd worn it in my honor, until Sylvie complained that she could rarely persuade him to wear anything else. They were planning an extended return to Australia, to study more Aboriginal artists.

"I can't wait to get back to the desert, to the light and the clear air," enthused Jean-Pierre. "Australia," he sighed. "It was a rebirth for me."

Down the table, their son Benjamin, now twelve years old, scowled. He needed another trip to Australia like the plague. Thanks to his parents' nomadic existence, he'd had enough rebirths in his short life, and he wanted to stay put. In Provence he had been identified by the government as a "hope of the region" in juvenile table tennis. Much to their astonishment, Jean-Pierre and Sylvie had raised a jock. I wondered if he'd caught the bug during his early exposure to Australia's sports-mad culture. Whatever the reason, "le ping-pong" was, to Benjamin, the meaning of life.

I thought of Janine's boys, their rock-solid daily routine, their steady small orbit of school and village. I wondered if Benjamin really would prefer that life. Or if Janine's boys would want to swap with him the chance to visit Indian reservations or to live in traditional Aboriginal communities.

For the first time, it occurred to me that my childhood had offered the best of both alternatives: the stability of a secure and reliable real world, and the infinite adventure of the invented one inhabited by my pen pals—those helpless ciphers on whom I had projected the fantasies of my imaginary life.

12

Breakfast with
the Queen of the Night

⁓❦⁓

I returned from Janine's quiet village in January 1996 with just one piece of my pen-pal puzzle still missing. The last person I had to find was the first to whom I'd written: Sonny Campbell—"Little Nell"—the older girl on the other side of Sydney who had the "brainwave" so many years earlier, "thinking you might like to be my pen-friend."

She should have been the easiest to contact. Unlike the others, I didn't have to track her down. I knew exactly where she was. And it was a long way from where she'd started. While her name wasn't in lights, it *was* on a very big awning in New York City.

"The magic is back. And its name is Nell."
In 1987, I was in Cairo between assignments, leafing through a months-old copy of *Vanity Fair*. Sometimes U.S. glossies made it past the ravages of the Egyptian censors. This time the lead sentence of a piece on New York night life com-

pelled me to flip back a page and study the Annie Leibovitz picture that accompanied the article. A leggy odalisque reclined on a velvet chaise. The article told how this striking woman had made a rat-infested electronics store into a nightclub named Nell's that had become the city's new hot spot. As the limos lined up outside the velvet-roped entrance, she had turned away Cher and made movie stars like Michael Douglas wait for admission. Mick Jagger, Warren Beatty and various exiled European princes vied for a nod from the fabulous propri-etress.

"[S]he reeks of Berlin 1930," wrote *Vanity Fair*'s Bob Co-lacello. "She wears black and red: short tight clothes that em-phasize her dancer's figure, backless dresses that expose her lovely pale skin. But there's a spark beneath her pallor, a sweet-water freshness that transcends her Cabaret chic. Despite her apparently febrile existence, Nell is a sensible, clean-living, hard-working kid from Sydney, Australia. . . ."

My pen pal had grown up to be crowned New York's new "queen of the night."

Nell's last letter to me, in July 1967, began with an apology: "Well, I'm ashamed of myself. I'm TERRIBLY sorry for not writ-ing for so long." She went on to list her onerous responsibilities: "school is awfully tough at the moment . . . exams . . . monthly tests . . . studying a lot . . . lots of ballet classes . . . rehearsals . . . having a concert soon." And then, the dreaded sentence: "Because of these reasons I don't think I can write to you anymore. . . . I have very much enjoyed receiving your letters. . . . I hope you find yourself another pen-friend more reliable than me."

I did, of course. Writing to Nell had been just the first chink in the door to a wider world; she had emboldened me to seek out the others who would allow me to kick it open.

After the letters stopped, I still heard about her, here and there. She left school at sixteen, as she'd planned, and spent a year in acting classes. Then, when her father got an assignment in his newspaper's London bureau, she went with him. Her big sister Sally was already in London. The two of them flatted together while Nell worked as a soda jerk, tap-dancing between tables and belting out show tunes. One of her customers was the director Jim Sharman, who cast her in *The Rocky Horror Show.* When the stage play later became a cult movie, Nell played the tap-dancing biker's moll who remains one of its icons.

And then I lost the plot of her story. I didn't know that she returned to Sydney from London in 1985, the same year I came home from the United States. And when I went off on assignment to the Middle East, she moved to New York. She took an apartment just a block from my old place on East Thirteenth Street.

But even though our tracks covered the same ground, we never met. I was shy about calling her; I suspected I wasn't quite cool enough to make it past the velvet ropes of her acquaintance. In 1996, when I finally picked up the phone and dialed her number, I realized it had been thirty years since our first exchange of letters.

The voice that answered was the voice of those silverfish-nibbled pages. Pickets of exclamation marks fenced her sentences. Word leaped suddenly into BOLD TYPE. Her accent seemed as hybrid as a Labradoodle or a Cockerpoo. Big round English vowels suddenly deflated into Aussie flatness with just a hint of Yankee drawl. It was like listening to Queen Elizabeth channeling Nicole Kidman.

Nell suggested we meet for breakfast. I was surprised; I hadn't imagined encountering the queen of the night in daylight. She proposed an East Village café right near my old apartment on Thirteenth Street. Sliding into the cab, I was delighted to hear the cabbie say it again: "Ya want Toideenth and Toid?"

The café faced what was once the Variety Vaudeville Theater—as apt a place as any to meet up with Nell. But the sign on the door said CLOSED TILL 11. It was just after nine. Apparently the queen of the night kept more conventional hours than the rest of her neighborhood.

While I waited for her, I wandered down the block to take a sentimental look at my old apartment. When I first arrived in New York, my school friend Kate, who was studying acting, had been living there and I'd been appalled by the overturned garbage in front of the stoop and the stink of urine in the foyer. In Sydney, even students could share houses in desirable neighborhoods, or find little flats like the one I'd had, with park views and a garden. "How could Kate live in a place like this?" I thought. A few months later, when I'd become better acquainted with the realities of Manhattan real estate, I begged her for a room.

Someone had given my old brownstone a coat of paint and put an intercom on the door. In my day, guests had to shout from the street if they wanted to be let in. The Spanish bodega was gone from the building next door. The rasping of its shutter had been my morning alarm clock. Now, it looked as if the street had priced itself out of reach of students and Hispanics.

It was a chilly, late winter morning. To keep my mind off the cold, I pulled a couple of Nell's letters from my bag and reread them as I waited. They reeked of our sun-drenched childhoods, of warm summer evenings and sticky school uniforms. Even her Sydney address, Coolabah Avenue, was enough to set the tune to "Waltzing Matilda" on auto-rewind in my brain:

Once a jolly swagman camped by a billabong,
Under the shade of a coolabah tree . . .

Standing there on that Manhattan street corner, the billabong stretched in front of me, red rocks reflecting in its limpid surface. Overhead, a flock of pink and gray galahs burst from the twisted branches of the coolabah tree and swirled into the burning blue of an Outback sky.

She had a dancer's walk: the slight turnout of the toes, the bounce on the balls of her feet. She wore a long sweater, leggings and a well-tailored hacking jacket. A slash of dark red lipstick accentuated the auburn of her signature bob. The *New York Times* was tucked under her arm. "My father's influence," she said. "He made me a newspaper junkie." Her most recently opened establishment, a little restaurant named The Kiosk on the Upper East Side, had a frieze of newspaper mastheads accenting the wallpaper.

We peered longingly into the cozy dimness of the closed café. There was a Starbuck's a block away, but when I suggested it as an alternative, Nell looked at me as if I'd proposed we drink hemlock instead of coffee. "Oh NO," she exclaimed, wrinkling her nose. "It's SOOOOO bland." Instead, we set off at her long-legged trot in search of something with the right atmosphere.

"Bruce Chatwin said EVERYONE should walk twenty miles a day," she declared, and it seemed we might have to go that distance to find something acceptable at such an unfashionable hour. But then she remembered the twenty-four-hour Café Orlin on St. Mark's Place. For its denizens, 9:30 A.M. was more likely to be the tail end of a very long night rather than the start of an ordinary morning.

Sure enough, the window table was occupied by two tall transvestites wearing fake tiger skin and hiding the night's ravages under polka-dot scarves and huge, Grimaldi-esque dark glasses. "The girls are HERE!" Nell exclaimed approvingly as one got out a bottle of watermelon nail polish to touch up a tired manicure.

As we sat down I pulled out the letter Nell had written to me back in May 1966, in which she boasted of her late-night pajama party—"We talked ALL night (sorry, a bit of exajuration (or however you spell it) there we got to sleep at 1.30 AM!)." She laughed—a throaty roar that reminded me of her sister Sally, sequestered with Darleen in the sanctum of the Big Sister's Bedroom while I hovered by the door, eavesdropping and trying desperately to get the joke.

For the best part of a decade Nell's life had been like a continuous pajama party. But instead of the relatively staid hour of 1:30 A.M., she rarely got to bed before five. "I'd wake up at five the next afternoon without seeing daylight," she said. Defying the short half-life of most New York clubs, Nell's had remained hot for years. She said it had been a relief when the celebrity tide finally ebbed. "The drinking, smoky rooms, very high heels, up till dawn . . . I was never really a party person, and the club was like a party every night."

I looked at her over the froth of my cappuccino and wondered why she was saying such a thing. If this woman wasn't a party person, who was? Perhaps she was adopting Australian camouflage, coloring herself marsupial gray. It's one thing to be queen of the night in New York, but Australians know a tumbril is always waiting.

As the club's pressures eased, she finally had some energy for other interests. She enrolled in art class ("I'd always be the last one there—hung over, wearing sunglasses") and met a fresh-faced blond sculptor named Eamon Roche, who had become her partner in life and work. Together they were about to open a Vietnamese restaurant. Although the space was still a building site, *Vogue*'s editor Anna Wintour had visited the curing concrete and dangling wires the day before—"wearing about $20,000 worth of clothes"—looking for a hot venue for a party for a celebrity "so big she can't say who it is." Nell wasn't sure the restaurant would be ready, but that was part of the allure: "Everyone in this town always wants to be first." A *Vogue* function would be an ideal opening, for Wintour would bring the models, and a sprinkling of models made a room look right to the rest of fashionable Manhattan.

It wasn't the career Nell had imagined for herself in those long-ago Sydney letters. But when the time came to launch herself as an actress, she'd found that she didn't have the temperament to sit through drizzly London winters, patiently auditioning for small parts. Instead of capitalizing on her high profile after the release of *The Rocky Horror Picture Show,* she'd run off to Norfolk with a romantic poacher—"a bit of a D. H. Lawrence fantasy, I'm afraid—all my clothes were stained with blood from hiding his dead pheasants in my pockets." When she did turn up for a rare audition, "It was, 'Take me as I am or not at all.' Just because my hair was Schiaparelli pink and I had a broad Australian accent didn't mean I couldn't play Jane Eyre."

The staid world of London theater hadn't seen it that way, and her acting career stalled. It had only just begun to revive. In 1994 she made her first stage appearance in almost a decade, playing a fading actress in a farce, *You Should Be So Lucky,* written by one of New York's most famous drag queens, Charles Busch. The role won her a New York Critics Circle nomination. Choice film cameos followed. But her biggest part remained The Fabulous Nell, hostess to the famous.

I wondered if she'd seen a lot of appalling behavior at the club. "NOT ENOUGH appalling behavior!" she roared. "I saw a lot more outrageousness when I was living with the poacher in Norfolk than I have here. There, you'd go to a dinner party and the thing would get ENTIRELY disorderly and the host would end up in bed with his best friend's wife. Here, famous people are all drinking PERRIER and worrying about what everyone thinks of them."

It was time to visit the new restaurant to see how work was progressing. Nell looked around for our waitress. She was seated at a nearby table, tucking into a muffin. "She's having BREAKFAST!" Nell gasped. It wouldn't happen at any of her establishments.

We grabbed a cab for the ride to West Houston. As we pulled away from the curb, Nell leaned forward and tapped the driver on a crisply pin-striped shoulder. "Can I just comment," she said, "on how wonderfully you're dressed?"

Stuck in traffic in the gray, treeless streets of downtown, we talked wistfully of Sydney. She said she'd had a perfect childhood. "We were so free, ranging around all those huge backyards." She compared it to the constrained, scheduled, indoor lives of her friends' children in Manhattan. "We adored our parents, but we never saw them except at mealtimes. Here, the kids and their parents are never out of each other's sight."

I wondered aloud whether our generation really did mark the end of the era when people thought they had to go away to prove themselves. There had been such an inevitability to it, like a tribal initiation. Sometimes you looked forward to leaving, sometimes you dreaded it, but whatever you felt, you knew the departure date would eventually come.

It came for me in early September 1982. It was Australian spring, the time of year when the jasmine is in full bloom, filling the soft air with fragrance. As the taxi carried me over the Harbor Bridge, sunlight sparkled off the water as if some profligate billionaire had scattered armloads of crushed diamonds.

At the airport, the Qantas flight attendant called my seat-row number for boarding just as the piped Musak in the gate lounge turned from some unrecognizable bubble-gum tune to "New York, New York." It seemed like an omen: "If I can make it there, I'll make it anywhere . . ."

That song wasn't written just for twenty-six-year-olds from

faraway Sydney. My father had wanted to make it in New York: among his oldest letters, I'd found one from a New York agent, replying with cautious encouragement to his query about whether he should come East. "You have the voice, and the looks," she wrote. "But you'll also need luck. . . ."

In the end, luck wasn't with him. In late 1936 he set off with the Jay Whidden band for a national tour that was to culminate in a big engagement in Manhattan. They played to raves in cities like Denver and Shreveport. But in San Antonio they were booked into a grand ballroom—the kind the band often played in Los Angeles. The smaller, touring ensemble didn't have a big enough sound to fill the space. They flopped. Their next engagement in New York City was canceled. The band headed home to California, and then on to Australia. "I never got to see the Statue of Liberty," my dad often said.

I saw it for him, my second night in New York, from the railing of a ferry boat, standing alongside that other monumental American icon, Walter Cronkite. The boat party was something Columbia Journalism School did every year, to welcome its incoming class. That night, as I stared up at the Brooklyn Bridge and the World Trade Center, I thought I'd never leave.

But my infatuation with New York City burned itself out like a brief affair. By the end of the year I was happy to go anywhere, even Cleveland. And Sydney shimmered in my memory like a glorious mirage.

When I go home to Sydney now, I visit friends who haven't seen any reason to leave. These days, their books get reviewed in the *New York Times,* their plays are staged in London, their screenplays are bought by Hollywood. One writes from his house on the harbor, and if his kids need to get to basketball practice, he ferries them there in the little speedboat parked at the end of his yard. And while it's no longer necessary to become an expatriate in order to find an international audience, the audience at home has become more interested in indigenous things. Talent doesn't have to be lauded elsewhere before it's acclaimed.

Nell's younger sister had become a prize-winning artist without leaving Sydney; just a few years earlier, a stint abroad in Paris or New York might have been required before Australians would have taken her work seriously. Her brother was a solar-energy scientist, doing his research at the University of New South Wales and exporting his expertise to remote Sudanese villages. Her older sister Sally had come home from London just as the Australian movie industry was beginning to flourish. One of her first credits, Animal Handler on *My Brilliant Career*, led to her own brilliant career in film production. One month she'd be in London, working on the Royal Albert Hall scenes in *Shine,* the next she'd be in the Outback, on a shoot with Ralph Fiennes in *Oscar and Lucinda.*

Nell's siblings lived within a few miles of each other and within walking distance of the beach. Sometimes, when she compared her life with theirs, she wondered if she'd stayed in Manhattan too long. "Do you think I could do this in Sydney?" she asked as the cab crawled through Soho traffic. Sure, I replied. I'd just read somewhere that Sydney had more restaurants per head of population than any city other than San Francisco. But she looked dubious. The Sydney she left, in the early seventies, was still a very small place. And when she went back, she spent her time in rushed visits to childhood friends. Her image of the city seemed colored by that more claustrophobic time.

And yet things kept happening that gave her doubts. Her old school, Abbotsleigh, had asked her to send a brief bio for an anniversary yearbook. She'd toiled over her entry. "I didn't want to be too . . . I didn't want to sound too . . ."

Too "tall poppy," perhaps?

"Well, I needn't have worried, because when I got the book

and read the lives that all my classmates have had, I was the dullest one in there!"

That night, at her club, she flitted from table to table as the room slowly filled. The club was in its tenth year—ancient for a New York night-life venue. And while the limos no longer disgorged roomfuls of celebrities, the place did a steady business as, among other things, the chief downtown redoubt of the city's stylish young black crowd.

"Over there, I think, was the blow job," said Nell, pointing an elegant, red-nailed index finger at a corner of the nightclub dance floor where a young woman allegedly performed oral sex on the rap star Tupac Shakur. "How *anyone* saw it I don't know. It's wall-to-wall bodies in here."

Nell no longer presided at the club every night. But she had an affection for the place that was evident as she wandered from floor to floor, plumping pillows on the sofas, adjusting the lighting levels, putting a tilted lampshade straight. She paused in the ladies' room to show off the "wallpaper"—hundreds of old postcards she shellacked herself back in the days when she and her partners were creating this fantasy of a British gentlemen's club.

"See how we did the stairs? When the oriental rugs get worn we cut them up and have them made into runners. You see that chandelier? It still gets dusted *every* day." Like Janine's tiny village, this place, too, had its routines, the small, unglamorous details that are the foundation of a larger-than-ordinary life.

When Nell reached the dance floor, she strutted and twirled across the polished boards. She wore a clingy leotard and a frothy tulle skirt that showed off the legs the *New York Times*'s drama critic in 1994 called the best "this side of a Folies-Bergère revue." The twelve-year-old who tap-danced at the breakfast table now had a dance floor of her very own.

I had planned to stay, to see out the night with her. But by midnight I was already tired, and the club had barely begun to come to life. I left her there, being fabulous, and began the journey home to a place where the last lights in town had probably gone out hours ago.

13

Yours, Faithfully

❦

There is no yellow mailbox at the end of my driveway anymore. The mailman doesn't come to us out here, in this tiny village at the foot of Virginia's Blue Ridge Mountains.

Instead, every morning, a little before noon, we go to the post office to pick up the mail. It's a pleasant walk, even when snow dusts the neighbors' hay bales and sits heavily on the wooded foothills rising to the west. When the weather starts to warm, the old Arabian stallion emerges from the barn opposite my house and rolls in the dirt like a puppy, four feet in the air, turning his silvery coat chocolate brown.

The post office is right in the center of the village, as it has been for more than a hundred years. Inside, there's a big table for sorting mail and a bench, for sitting. Neighbors linger to exchange gossip or scan the notice board for what's going on in the village. Usually that's not too much, which is pretty well how we like it.

The mail in my box is mostly the modern clutter of catalogues, bills and telephone-company solicitations. Most of it goes straight into the big recycling bin by the table. But among the letters I carry home are a few that remind me of my father's eclectic daily haul. There are stamps from the new Palestine Authority, postmarks from Nigeria and Iran. Other letters, from Kurdistan or Sarajevo, have been hand-carried out of chaos and mailed from Ankara or Vienna.

These days the writers aren't pen friends, just old acquaintances from a life I've left behind. Raed, from the West Bank, stoned my car in 1987; now he writes to tell me how he's faring in college. Deebi helped me when I was thrown in jail in Nigeria; now he writes despairing news about death sentences on his fellow environmental activists. Nazaneen was a brilliant teacher from a wealthy family when I met her during the Kurdish uprising after the war with Iraq. Now she's a refugee, working long hours selling vegetables in a London suburb. And I am no longer a Foreign Correspondent, just someone who corresponds with foreigners.

Unless civil war breaks out for a second time in Virginia, it is unlikely that I will ever see a battlefield again. These days I don't cover uprisings or get arrested on suspicion of espionage. I bake bread, piece quilts, turn the compost heap and sit on the porch, rocking my son to sleep. The place I live has less than half the population of St. Martin de la Brasque, and a letter can find me here with just the name of the village as address. Of all my pen pals, it is Janine's whose life now most resembles mine.

My father was appalled when I moved back to the United States in 1993. Ten years earlier, when I was studying in New York, he had written me a long letter lamenting Darleen's expatriation, hoping that she would never forget she was "born an Aussie, when Aussies were true Aussies." He warned me of the debilitating materialism of the United States—"I forecast what's happening (damn my country of birth!) 20 or more years ago"—and wrote about the beginnings of his love affair with Australia.

"In the big war it was amazing. My Yank brothers were lost without their tools, their mobile kitchens and fresh food supplies. We Aussies made do, we extemporized. The only way to stop these Aussies doing something progressive was to encase them in a block of cement. . . . Odd stuff coming from an ancestry that on three sides was [in the United States] before 1776—but that's it, I'm only sorry I wasn't born an Aussie."

His Australian patriotism had become almost a religious faith, and it pained him when Darleen and I both "married out." He was sure, when I brought my American husband home, that Tony would see Australia as he had, and settle thankfully into life as an Aussie bloke. But Tony, born in Washington, D.C., had grown up witnessing major news stories unfold on his doorstep: civil rights and antiwar marches, the rioting following Martin Luther King's assassination, Watergate. As a reporter in Sydney, he found it hard to adjust to Australia's quieter politics or to muster much passion over its less acute social problems. The fairness that made Australia such a decent place to live also made it, for him, an unsatisfying place to work. After a sweet three years in our little sandstone cottage near the harbor in Balmain, he was restless. And when the offer of the Middle East posting was dangled in front of us, I had to admit that somewhere deep inside I was, too.

Six years later it was Tony's turn to be homesick, and it seemed only fair that we should spend some time near his family. We found this village in the foothills of the Blue Ridge, and to my surprise I began to feel settled here in a way that I never had in any place other than Sydney.

Even though Tony had traded in his foreign-correspondent khakis for the sports coat of a national reporter, I was still working for the foreign desk. I'd developed a skill in dealing with chaotic situations and had become what's known in newsrooms as a fireman, or, less politely, a "shit-hole correspondent"—a person dispatched to cover the worst of places in the worst of times.

At first I thought our Blue Ridge village would be a perfect base for a fireman-foreign correspondent, a tranquil retreat in between hectic assignments. But after a year, the village's very peacefulness proved my undoing. Instead of craving risk, I craved quiet. Each trip, getting out the door became harder and harder. Under fire in Somalia, I'd find myself thinking of my shipment of autumn perennials, worrying whether Tony would know what to do with them if they arrived before I got home. In my years on the road, I had run up a domesticity deficit. And the time between assignments was never enough to balance the books.

A light snow was falling as I packed for a flight to Bosnia. Journalists were getting shot there, and I was worried that the military camouflage on the helmet I was taking would make me look too much like a combatant. After puzzling over the problem for a while, I figured that if I stretched a pair of black panty hose over the helmet and tied the legs together on top, in a bow, it would cover the camouflage and at least give a sniper pause if he had me in his sights.

The phone rang as I was stuffing the helmet into a duffel bag. The voice on the other end was my mother's: a terrible, broken voice I'd never heard before. There had been other calls through the long course of my father's illness. I had flown home, thinking each time that it would be my last chance to hold his fragile hand. But my mother's iron will had pulled him through crisis after crisis. Now, her spent voice told me that she'd finally had to let him go.

The last flight to Australia that day left at 5 P.M. and it was already after three. "You'll never make it," the travel agent said. But making unmakable flights was part of my job description. As Tony read a credit card number into the phone, I tossed the bulletproof vest and the down-filled parka out of my bag and threw in a few light dresses for Sydney's midsummer. Tony drove wildly through the snow until traffic snarled at the ramp to Dulles Airport's departure lounge. I jumped from the car and sprinted the last icy half mile to the terminal, barged through the check-in queue and ran to the gate. As the plane door closed behind me, I finally began to cry.

"And when did you last see your father?" the British writer Blake Morrison asks himself repeatedly in the memoir that chronicles the life and loss to cancer of the "domineering old sod" who shaped his life. Was it when his father last smiled? When he last did something for himself unaided? When he last felt healthy? "I keep trying to find the moment when he was last unmistakably there, in the fullness of his being, *him*," Morrison writes. Morrison finds the answer in a weekend visit when his father was still well enough to drive from his home in Yorkshire to London, to offer unsolicited handyman help in his son's newly acquired house. Bickering gently as they had always done, they hung a chandelier, repaired curtain rails, mounted shelves. In the meticulous doing of these small tasks, Morrison finds the essence of the man who was his father.

When I read Morrison's book, almost a year after my father's death, I tried to find my own answer to the question. I'm not sure I can. In the way that Morrison means, I may never have seen my father at all.

In 1982, when I was writing the application that would win the scholarship to Columbia University, I had to say why I'd decided to be a journalist. I described the day I'd visited my father at his Sydney newspaper office. He'd taken me down to the pressroom just before a print run. There was bustle, tension. The giant presses thumped to life, slowly at first, then faster, the huge spools of newsprint spinning into a blur, the floor shuddering, the noise gathering like rolling thunder. He reached onto the conveyor and gave me a paper. It was warm in my hand. Hot off the presses. I was one of the first to read the latest news. And I knew it was my father's love of words and skill with them that made sure it reached the street clear and readable, free of errors.

I gave the Columbia application to him, as usual, to correct the grammar and spelling. I thought my description of how he'd influenced me would flatter him. But his expression, when he returned it marked up with the usual scrawls, was sad and wry. "There was a time," he said, "when I was a lot more than a proofreader."

He wanted me to remember him as a famous young singer. But I couldn't, because that was a life he had before I was old enough to have memories.

That life had emerged for me in fragments, disinterred a piece at a time as I grew old enough to be trusted with the answers to baffling questions. I was in my teens when I first saw my birth certificate and realized that Lawrie Brooks hadn't always been my father's name. The story was that a dull name like Bob Cutter wasn't memorable enough for a performer. Daddy said he'd looked out his agent's office window and seen a Brooks Brothers store across the street. At that moment he jettisoned the names his forebears had carried to the New World in the 1700s and adopted, instead, the name of a brand of preppy clothing.

Years later, when I was much older, he added a new twist to the story. Instead of the name Bob Cutter not being memorable enough, he confided that it had become *too* memorable to certain influential people in Hollywood. A woman named Ruby—the glamorous woman in the red sequined sheath whose photograph had so intrigued me as a child—had fallen for Bob Cutter in his white tuxedos and black silk shirts. Ruby was the wife of a powerful movie director. Bob Cutter was also married at the time. Their romance—and the divorces that followed—titillated Hollywood, enraged Ruby's husband and his friends, and put a brake on Bob Cutter's career.

The divorces also robbed a toddler of her daddy. There *was* a daughter old enough to have the memories he wished upon me. Morneen Kamiki, the Hawaiian-born child of Bob Cutter's first marriage, was there when thousands danced to his songs in the grand ballrooms. But the daddy she remembers was only a smiling stranger who visited a few times; a voice on the radio, a handsome creature who waved goodbye and went off to never-never land to live with the other fairy princes and princesses.

Once she was old enough to realize that never-never land was Bland Street, Ashfield, she wrote to him—her "Daddy Bob" in faraway Australia. I didn't realize that many of the fat foreign letters in the mailbox, or the beautiful picture books of California wilderness that arrived each Christmas, were from her. All this mail was simply attributed to "relatives in America." My parents were trying to protect me from the small minds of neighbors and nuns who equated divorce with damnation. And I suppose they were right. I was worried enough about my father not being a Catholic. If I'd known he was a *divorced* non-Catholic my anxiety would have been unbearable.

My mother learned about Lawrie's daughter during his tram-ride proposal of marriage back in 1946. Gloria's strong maternal feelings were stirred by the prospect of caring for this little girl. She urged him to try for custody as soon as they were married, and was disappointed when he said that, after so many years away, he had no right to uproot a child to whom he was little better than a stranger.

Later he bridged that estrangement as best he could in an honest and lifelong correspondence. When I was old enough, he shared some of her letters with me. When Miki and I finally met, as adults, it was easy for us to recognize each other as sisters.

Scientists have discovered that all human beings have a "happiness set point"—that just as our bodies have a preset weight to which they will tend to return after diet or binge, our minds are preprogrammed at a certain level of contentment. Thus, the mood-altering effects of winning a Pulitzer or losing a spouse will rarely endure. Within a year, most people are again either the happy or morose persons they always were. Therefore, the researchers suggest, the pursuit of happiness may be more successful if we give up hoping for triumphs and instead sprinkle our lives with whatever small gratifications—working in the garden, eating a favorite food—give us day-to-day pleasure. A writer named Steven Lewis puts this eloquently in his book *Zen and the Art of Fatherhood.* It is, he writes, between the bread and the butter that the great moments of life are lived.

Lewis also observes that children are naturally Zenlike in their games, living entirely in the here and now. But I was not a Zenlike child. My games were never of here, always of elsewhere. My pen pals were extensions of those childhood games.

And now one of them is dead, one is famous, one has survived wars, one overcome prejudice. And of all of them, it is Janine, living undramatically in the narrow circumference of her tiny village, whose life now seems to me most enviable. Never emerging from her warm cocoon, content with the slight satisfactions of preparing a tasty daube or being there each afternoon to see the small, smiling face that emerges from the school bus, she nourishes her happiness set point. A life's great moments, lived between the *baguette* and the *beurre.*

.   .   .

I wish I could tell my father that I'm glad I knew him as settled, predictable Lawrie Brooks and not as wild, young Bob Cutter. I know I am much luckier to have been born to the forty-eight-year-old who was soon to give up the triumphs of fame and applause. The father I knew had time to make hash browns and flapjacks of a Saturday morning and to sprinkle his life with the pleasures of a cricket ball well bowled or a backyard lawn fresh-mown.

When I was in New York he wrote to me, describing the metamorphosis of Bob Cutter into Lawrie Brooks. "After a couple of glamour-girl marriages and a hell of a lot of fun in between," he wrote, he'd married "the most wonderful, the most restrictive, the most respected woman" he'd ever met in his life. "Took me ten years to completely realize what a treasure I had, but, believe me, that feeling has only grown with these 36-plus years."

I was born in the ninth year of their marriage. When he gave up singing five years later, I was too young to question it. Later I assumed it was because of his stage fright. When I asked, he said he hated the way some performers kept going past their prime. He wanted to stop while he was still singing at his best. He was fifty-four.

But filling out the forms required by his death, I found an old copy of his own father's death certificate from the Salvation Army home in Los Angeles. Hard living had killed Winthrop Cutter at the age of fifty-four. It seemed too much of a coincidence to suppose that his own father's death wasn't on Lawrie's mind when he reached that age. He often said that if it hadn't been for meeting my mother he would have been dead in his fifties.

Instead, the coffin draped with the Australian flag contained the body of a man just a few days shy of his eighty-seventh birthday.

My mother, my sister and I each brought a single Australian flower—spiky green banksia, glossy red protea, the spidery bloom of yellow grevillia—and laid them on the deep blue ground of the flag. An old army mate gave the eulogy, ending with a description of his last visit to see Daddy in hospital. "I left him listening to the cricket match," he said. "I'm glad he went while the Aussies were still ahead."

As everyone else filed out to begin the wake, Mummy turned back and walked to the head of the coffin. She bent down and patted it gently. "You're all right now," she whispered. "You're all right now."

Daddy would have liked the wake: his voice certainly would have swelled the rising noise level as the wine, beer and whiskey flowed. Occasionally someone glanced out the window at the darkening sky. It was a Friday afternoon, a day that would become infamous in Sydney as Black Friday. The city was burning; bush fires from north, south and west had raged right into the heart of the leafy suburbs. Later, when everybody else had left, the three of us sat in the garden as burned leaves fluttered down on the hot wind and settled, blackened, on the grass.

They were evacuating houses a few miles away. Our house, entirely timber, was surrounded by a copse of native trees that my sister and I planted the year my parents moved here. Red gums, scribbly barks, spotted gums and iron barks dangled twisted boughs over the iron roof. They were eucalyptus, parched by a hard summer. If the fire reached them they would explode like torches. There would be no saving the house. Mummy, lost in grief, was apathetic. "Let it burn," she said.

But the fires turned and took their tragedy to other families. We went inside to sleep. It was the first time in our lives that the three of us had ever been together alone. Until then, there had always been at least one husband present.

• • •

Early one afternoon a week later, the funeral parlor called. They had Daddy's ashes. Darleen and I drove down to the funeral parlor and collected the box. It was oblong, cardboard, and surprisingly heavy. Inside was a plastic bag with a twist-tie.

We turned the car north, toward the most beautiful of the pink sand beaches. It was raining at last, a fine mist that fell like a salve on the stricken bushland. Across Pittwater, faint columns of smoke rose from blackened tree stumps as the rain doused the last of the smoldering embers.

I knew those dry coastal forests; I knew they had already begun their recovery. The fire had split open ancient seed pods that had waited years for their moment to germinate. The blasted gums would shed their injured skins as easily as a model shrugging off a jacket. And in just a few days the cabbage-tree palms would send tender new green leaves straight out of their roasted, lifeless-looking trunks. But the whole process seemed so extravagant, designed by a careless and profligate god.

I glanced at the box of ash on the seat between us. There was waste there, too. I thought of all the things my father learned in his long life: how to pick up the sheet music for a song he'd never heard and perform it perfectly; when to replace a fused participle with a possessive and a gerund; how to be a father to the best of his ability. A line from Wilfred Owen's poem "Futility" ran through my head.

Was it for this the clay grew tall?
Oh, what made fatuous sunbeams toil to break earth's sleep at all?

When we got out of the car, the sea air had an unusually brisk edge for a midsummer's day. We had thought to give his ashes to the sea, the rolling Pacific that bracketed the beginning of his life as a towheaded boy in California, and its end as a frail old man on a bed by a picture window in Sydney. But at the far end of the beach, where the land rises in soft dunes to a hard nob of rocky bushland, we noticed a piece of fallen cliff: a huge cube of sandstone sundered as if an angry giant had brought down his fist and smashed it in two. It was impossible to imagine a grander headstone.

The wind was raw on the headland. We climbed higher as the misty rain swirled and the surf reached for us, its tendrils of white foam curling up the rock face. When we were above the giant V of the split, we pulled out his last whiskey bottle. We each drank a shot, toasting his life. We poured the ashes down the golden sandstone, and the rest of the whiskey after them. The rain and the salt spray carried them far away.

ABOUT THE AUTHOR

Geraldine Brooks is the author of *Nine Parts of Desire*. A native of Australia and a graduate of Sydney University and the Columbia University Graduate School of Journalism, she lives in Virginia with her husband and son.